The Break

Also by Steven Paul Lansky

Jack Acid, an audio novel
Main St., poems
Eleven Word Title for Confessional Political Poetry Originally Composed for Radio, poems
A Black Bird Fell Out of the Sky
Life is a Fountain

THE BREAK

a memoir

Steven Paul Lansky

ARBITRARY PRESS
New York

Grateful acknowledgment is made to the following publications in which some of
the material in this book appeared, albeit in a slightly different form: *St. Petersburg
Review, Streetvibes, The Brooklyn Rail, Artspike, Article 25, and Citybeat*

ArbitraryPressBooks.com

2 4 6 8 9 7 5 3 1

First Edition

Dona. Maggie. Len.

What's madness but nobility of soul at odds with circumstance? The day's on fire!

--Theodore Roethke

CONTENTS

Prologue   1

Part 1   7

1. Stone Soup   9

2. Lacey #1   15

3. Lacey #2   19

4. Wailing Wheels   27

5. Lacey #3   29

6. Lacey #4   37

7. Don't Wear Sandals #5 The Film   39

8. Leaving NYC on the NJ Train   47

9. Crisis Central   53

10. Trenton State Hospital   55

11. Into Steady Meditations   63

12. Lacey #5   73

13. My Feet Are Two Different Sizes   77

14. Burlington and Beyond   83

Part 2   89

15. Rigo, My Brother, My Brother   91

16. Rigo and His Wife, Afraid   95

17. Customs   99

18. I Will Stop and Put Them Off   109

19. Lacey #6   113

20. He Was Frozen in Time   115

21. I Watched a Girl Dance   119

22. Beyond Binghamton   127

23. Afraid I'd Leave a Mark   133

24. Pittsburgh—July 10, 2001   141

Part 3   147

25. Dark-eyed Amy   149

26. Cycling Up Salem Road   151

27. Columbus Love Tap   157

28. Kelly and the Cigarette   161

29. Buying the Look   165

30. Smoking Is Only Allowed in the Back   171

31. Darke County Days   181

32. To Convince Even the Grebe and Goose   195

33. L'Oiseau de Feu, Tom & Mickey   201

34. White Wolf's Way   203

35. Paranoia or Hate Campaign   213

36. Hospital Days   217

Epilogue   231

Acknowledgments   236

Prologue

In my journal entry of April 4th, 2001, I wrote: "Today begins the Geodon experiment."

I don't know why, but while I was in the middle of it, I didn't know what was happening to me or connect it to the Geodon. Maybe I didn't want to know.

Here's more from my journal:

> It's the third day with a half dose of Haldol. I am taking two point five milligrams at bedtime (which is often early in the morning) plus twenty milligrams of Geodon. This is the newest atypical anti-psychotic. I've been taking it for over a week, and now I'm beginning to gradually reduce the older, tranquilizing Haldol. What's different? I'm waking up earlier and with slightly more energy and clarity. Right now, I'm at Sitwell's coffeehouse at three on a Saturday afternoon. It's blustery, warm, and the sky is full of pollen, petals, and seeds. I'm praying that I can get some more grading done than is usual for me on a Saturday afternoon. I think I'm pumping the energy gained (if there is such a thing) into career channels. Over the last week, I've done a little more cleaning and caretaking at home, though at this end of the semester rush, it seems obvious that I must balance major work demands with other needs. I've recently started drinking Red Rose tea, a black

tea made from orange pekoe. The caffeine starts
my afternoon. It also helps break up the phlegm, as
I'm recovering from a head and chest cold.

The fact is, that when this story begins in the spring of 2001,
I was 43-years-old, an age at which presumably I should have
had a better understanding of my condition and its perils. Yet
I was surprisingly full of optimism, dismissive of the idea that
things might take a bad turn for me because I'd decided to try a
different kind of medication. Like most people suffering from
schizophrenia, my natural capacity to read behavioral signs,
either in myself or others, was often impaired. It was, in my
case, a condition that had not been diagnosed until I was nearly
20. This was not at all unusual. Schizophrenia doesn't usually
present until the late teens. Onset in males tends to happen in
late adolescence during the period when teens emancipate from
their parents.

Growing up in Cincinnati with my parents, Len and
Dona, a social psychologist and a piano teacher, and my
older brother Rigo, I had endured the normal bumps and
agonies of adolescence. I was a precocious kid, sometimes
difficult and argumentative (especially when I felt wronged
or misunderstood—which was perhaps more often than
warranted). I was also articulate and intellectual, a good student,
popular with my peers. I worked hard and managed to graduate
high school a year early, gaining admittance to Harvard as a
legacy.

At 17, I was an adventurer who loved cycling, driving, and
sailing. I was something of an athlete and an aspiring polymath.
But I had also begun drinking alcohol and smoking pot. I had
a contentious relationship with my father, who could go from
nasty to nice in the blink of an eye. Often, I found myself angry
with what I perceived as his undue criticisms. I was frightened
by the level of my anger.

Before beginning my freshman year at Harvard, I
cycle-camped with my brother, Rigo, and some friends from
Cincinnati to Cambridge. We pedaled for several weeks in
different groups and combinations. We were a co-ed group, and
the social dynamics were a real challenge for me. One of the
girls went with Rigo. We got into arguments, and I cried. The trip
took us to Ann Arbor, Burlington, Vermont, and East Barrington,

New Hampshire. As well, it carried me to the limits of emotional instability. My agreement with my father had been that I would not ride alone. But in the end, I rode alone several times. Being alone grew on me.

Arriving at Harvard, I grew my hair long and went to live in the Dudley Co-Op, an alternative housing option that attracted campus misfits. The Co-Op breathed with counter-cultural energy. A half-painted rising sun and an outlined Mao Tse Tung adorned a stairwell wall. I met people who had lived in India, one who had served in Vietnam, one who'd been an extra in the movie *Jaws*. Painted on one wall was the figure of Pogo, the cartoon possum, with the caption "Round here, Cleanliness is Next to Madness!" Several Co-Opers actually did go mad that year, were carted off in straitjackets or returned home for an extended break, never to return. Not me. I worked hard and made Dean's list. The summer following freshman year, I went back to Cincinnati and apprenticed myself to a cabinetmaker. I found the work honest but unfulfilling. I had become convinced that I was meant to live the life of an artist. The hobo musical tradition, the Beat writers, the free and nomadic life—this, I felt certain, was my calling.

My family disagreed. But I was stubborn. Instead of going back to Harvard in the fall, I decided to spend the year traveling. I hitchhiked to California. I told stories in coffeehouses and bars. I picked up the harmonica. I began smoking marijuana and drinking with increasing gusto.

I thought I was well adjusted, but the marijuana hit me hard. I realize now how much it affected me, though the extent to which it contributed to my illness is unclear. What is clear is that what started as a fun thing for me became something else.

With schizophrenia, there is no insight into when the hallucinations occur. The intoxicating nature of the emotional euphoria makes living seem magical and funny in ways that obviate fear. Years later, when I got into therapy and tapered off marijuana and alcohol, I became better able to accept the severity of my anxiety and discomfort and grew more comfortable in my own skin. When I stopped drinking, the voices in my head went away. While I reject the idea that my addictions led to schizophrenia or that I self-medicated to cover up my affliction, there's really no way to know. What I do know is that once the label of schizophrenia is applied, there is no turning back from it. There will always be those who doubt that I am really mentally ill when seeing me function competently at a job, manage a sober living, or form meaningful relationships. At such times, I, too, can begin to doubt that I have an illness. Schizophrenia has no blood test, no brain image scan, no truly objective criteria for diagnosis. Yet it is cross-cultural, and roughly one percent of the population is so afflicted.

My decision not to return to Harvard was certainly not evidence in and of itself of madness. Still, in combination with other things that were going on, it raised questions about my stability. I had trouble with the friend that I cycled across Wyoming with. We got into a love triangle with an older woman. He talked to Rigo about it, and when I, drunk and stoned, pushed the woman, she talked to Rigo, too. Then, after five days spent walking and hitchhiking from San Francisco, and with my feet bleeding, there came the Rolls Royce protest, where I took a joyride in a car left at a turnaround with keys in it on the day after a big Marijuana Smoke-in on the grounds of the Lincoln Memorial. The only I.D. I carried on the joyride was an indigent's Medical Card from a hospital in New Orleans I had visited when I stayed with the Harë Krishnas after Mardi Gras. I was charged with the unauthorized use of a motor vehicle. After I landed in the city jail, the attorney retained for me by my family arranged to have me transferred to Spring Grove State Mental Hospital. A psychiatrist there tested me with an MMPI (Minnesota Multiphasic Personality Inventory) and concluded I had schizophrenia.

Later I was transferred, with the help of the same lawyer, to the Sheppard Pratt Mental Health facility in Baltimore, where the staff seemed torn between respecting my parent's request not to medicate me and protecting me from them. Pratt was an amazing facility, and while there, I listened to the Grateful Dead, read a beautiful ancient book by Leonardo da Vinci, swam alone in an Olympic pool, and was named chess champion of my floor. But when the therapy groups talked about suicide, I became angry and scared and did not want to talk about it. And when my lawyer encouraged me to admit that I had made a mistake with the Rolls, I maintained that it had been a protest and I was justified. When, despite that, I earned enough trust to go on an outing in Towson, I simply walked away, hitchhiking in the Airforce flight suit I'd bought at an Army Surplus store to my family's cabin in Ontario. At the Canadian border, the driver who'd given me a lift said to the customs agent, "He's a hitchhiker. I picked him up a few hours ago." And from there, things began to unravel. After the police were summoned, I was handcuffed and taken to another facility near Gananoque, where I spent a week and a half before my parents could once again intercede, this time taking me home.

It didn't take long before I was back in an institution. I lifted a chair in a threatening way in my mother's presence, and she called the authorities on me. In Probate Court, Mom took the stand and said that I had threatened her. My denial went deep, but I realized I was pretty ill. When I took the stand, all I could say was, "What she said is the truth."

The next five years of my life were spent in and out of psychiatric hospitals, short term and long term, private and public, as well as a year in two different group homes, one in Columbus, Ohio, one in Cincinnati. I needed time by myself to explore painting, sculpting, and drawing before I could accept the social help that my parents and the psychiatrists offered. I gradually accepted the rules and the medication. I managed to attend Ohio State University, starting part-time for about two years. I studied French, and English, and painted on my own. At the hospital, my artwork was encouraged. The therapeutic Expressive Arts Therapy is not to be confused with making art. But I did that too. I did both. Making sculpture, the tedious, methodical dialogue with the stone, and the requirement of the staff that I relate it to my recovery frustrated me, but it also grew my emotional accessibility. I intellectualized in relationships. Still do. I had a girlfriend that I met in a therapy group after being advised not to date anyone from treatment. I don't trust any of my memories of that relationship. I had good times and bad, but I have no remaining friends from that period of my life. I became adjusted to taking antipsychotic medicine.

When I was first diagnosed and titrated to my long-term and current dosage of the antipsychotic medication Haldol, the dose was too low to be considered therapeutic. Since then, the literature has adjusted to accept this lower dose as a common treatment. But Haldol, though it proved effective in stabilizing my condition, had a host of unpleasant side effects, including extreme drowsiness, tremors, loss of sex drive, constipation, and a general lassitude and lack of energy. I didn't want to be medicated. I craved freedom. I had been married for a time, but it had ended in divorce, and I craved a romantic companion even though I felt handicapped by my limitations. One of the common side effects of Haldol was a visible shake. I took another medication, Cogentin, to counteract the tremors, but they were only reduced, not eliminated. This symptom was annoying not only because of the physical manifestation but because of the resulting social anxiety, the having to explain it. Once the question was posed--"Why is your hand shaking?"—it prompted other, more complicated concerns: *Do I mention that it's caused by my medication? Does that mean I should explain my illness? What if this interaction could lead to a friendship? A sexual partner? A relationship?*

It was all very tricky. But was it fair not to tell? Changing medications wasn't going to eliminate that complicated question. And yet the promise of trying something new, something different, that might give me back essential parts of myself like energy and ambition (and eliminate unwanted side effects like tremors and a lumbering heaviness of movement and thought)—that was too tempting to pass up.

So, in April of 2001, I began my Great Geodon Experiment. I didn't know where it would take me, where it would lead. I'm calling the pages that follow a memoir, though perhaps, due to the chemistry of my brain, that description should be taken with a grain of salt (a bit of mental health humor there). By whatever designation, it's an account that is as true as I could make it, and I hope will prove illuminating and give a window into that time in my life and the fragile state I think of as sanity.

Steve Lansky
Cincinnati, 2022

PART 1

Steven 3.24.20

1

Stone Soup

A RAINY DAY IN Clifton after a long spring drought. Maybe because it was raining, I walked toward Ludlow Avenue under my blue umbrella, holding the wooden cane handle, my head full of worries: Reagan's Alzheimer's disease, Donna's problem with Mayor Rudy, the riots in downtown Cincinnati and a thousand other things too. I'm not sure why I decided to go to lunch at Tink's on Telford. But a man has to eat, and a lunch for reconnaissance at the most expensive restaurant in Clifton might be an excusable adventure, funded out of my graduate school stipend and loan. My mom, who was retired and had funds, had offered to take me to Tink's, with its leaded glass windows, awnings, and hardwood floors, but she wasn't able on this day, so I went without her. I'd only seen Tink's from the outside. I'd been afraid to go in because it was a proper establishment, and I was an impoverished grad student. But I wanted a bowl of hot soup on a rainy day even if I couldn't afford to go to New York City for the New Yorker Festival.

Entering, I recalled how when I was nineteen years old, on a cold January day just after New Year's 1978; I had gone to New York to personally deliver a typeset excerpt of my writing to *The New Yorker* magazine. On my way to the magazine's hallowed offices, I decided to detour to New York's stalwart Trinity Church despite not being Catholic. Growing up in provincial Midwest Cincinnati, I had mostly been exposed to Judaism (at drunken high holy days) and then later to Zen Buddhism on the Left Coast. But at that crucial moment, I had felt the need to embrace any God who might listen. Inside the church, it was quiet. The ceiling rose heavenward, and everything around me glowed with a golden hue. There were only a few people there besides me in the quiet afternoon of a weekday.

I knelt in my blue jeans and prayed—Oh, please, let me be published, and let her—the woman I wanted—let *her* love me. I spoke these words aloud in the vast empty church, my quiet young man's voice no more than a whisper. Then I went outside again—bundled against the cold gray city—and heard no music, no angel's bells, nothing but the cars, taxis, buses, honking, footsteps, swooshes, growls, engines, sweeping me along. And I walked and walked, taking in the grayness—until suddenly the neon sign of a pink open palm beckoned me. *Psychic Reader.* I went to the door. A woman leaned toward me, her head wrapped in a dark scarf, her eyes bulging and brown. She ushered me into an overheated room past a hanging curtain of yellow and pink paisley. I could hear children talking in the dark.

She told me to sit, turned on the table lamp, and asked, "Do you want the cards? To ask the cards?"

"Yes, yes," I said.

"It will be thirty-five dollars," she said. "And candles, you need candles."

I said, "Okay," a little reluctant, taking off my blue hat and plaid scarf. I shuffled my wet feet, watched as a brown puddle formed around my boots on the tile floor. "How much for candles?"

"Another ten," she said.

I took out my wallet. I had eighty dollars, and I gave her forty-five. She took the money quickly, lit candles, her hands moving deftly with the wooden matches. She sat across the card table. The yellow tablecloth had crumbs on it. Her eyes bulged as she untied a red scarf from around the Tarot deck. Her hands had a ring on every finger, all gold in color—the nails were long and pale pink.

"This is very good! You rule your own situation! The card was the emperor." She turned cards slowly now and emphasized again and again that I was sure to get everything. "Is there a girl? She loves you as much as you love her. And money—money will come to you. I see great success—a leader!" She put down the deck. "Do you want more candles? You will need many candles!"

I got up, pulled my pack with me, put on my hat and gloves, and edged toward the door.

"Okay, okay, okay," she said, her hands flashing gold and shiny pink. And then I was back on the cold dark street.

All these years later, I still wanted to publish in *The New Yorker*, and I would have been glad to present at their festival if they had promised to take my poem, *Gogol's Ear*, and paid for my train ticket and given me enough to book a hotel for two nights. I'd have sat on any panel, danced on any stage. I'd have even brought a harmonica and pretended I could blow for a dollar a day. That's more than I could make in Cincinnati. I mean that, ask any musician what it takes to get a dollar a day in Clifton. But no one invited me, no one asked, what's little Stevie Lansky doing this May? Why don't he come to New York for our little festival?

So, with this song of lamentation blowin', I pulled on the door handle of the loneliest restaurant in all of Clifton. The newest, richest, most exclusivest, nicest, fanciest, expensivest, poshest, bestest restaurant in all of Clifton. And it was easy to get in, but getting out, only a window of opportunity . . . that's all I asked. I had been on the phone all day trying to secure some university support to travel through the South on the New River train, into Washington, DC where the Federal Government seems to be located, where I'd change trains. But no calls came back that day, nor the next. Did that mean I was to abandon the adventure? Give up the dream of seeing Tracy Chapman or poetry in Bryant Park?

I called a professor and begged him to accompany me. I asked a friend. I called another friend and left a message with his daughter—all for naught. But lunch, that I could make happen. I'd have lunch at Tink's and regret I'd ever laid eyes on *The New Yorker* magazine, regret that I'd listened when my mother said, "Did you see the article in the *Times*?" Why had I listened to her? Me, stupid me, actually reading that big article about The New Yorker Festival, and thinking, Man, is this a story about temptation or what? It's not like I was reading the advertising. I was a poet. Not a good one, but all the same I'd been rated, discussed, envied, hated, reviewed, even praised once or twice, not only by younger persons but indeed even by a generation advanced in literacy who would call Bob Dylan a disrespectful Yank and Yank Rachell a respectable Negro. I went into Tink's with a bit of ambivalence, as I could easily have gone to a place where I knew what to expect. Let's trace the ambivalence back a few years to my first published poem circa 1983 in *The Art Academy News.* Here it is:

> POPSICLE STICK
> There's little left
> to kid about
> waiting in discouraged
> faced line gritting
> teeth against another
> cigarette smoked
> too quickly. The
> agony of it all
> escapes into huffs
> of white smoke to
> get food stamps
> under fluorescent lamps
> among the distraught
> faces of poor.
> Lines.
> Lines look like
> poetry, impoverished
> on a page, never
> short enough to
> say in even breaths,
> nor long enough
> to last
> all
> day.
> Like a popsicle melting
> and falling off the
> stick. What's left
> to lick tastes
> like the stick,
> wooden, but still
> a little bit
> sweet.

I suppose, if I eventually did arrive in New York City, I would get a lot of what I expected, and some of what I didn't. But at a

New York-style restaurant in Clifton, I didn't even know where I was supposed to sit. All the elderly women were two or three to a table. What I needed was to speak to a manager. I didn't want to appear eager, didn't want to be where I didn't belong. I'd lived in Clifton all my life, save fourteen years. I was almost 44. I knew the man the restaurant was named for.

The pasty-faced chubby blonde woman at the counter told me I could order at the counter, have a seat, and she'd bring my food. I asked her who did the artwork hanging on the walls. Two oil paintings, too yellow for my taste, but I didn't mention that. Another woman, the one at the register, told me the chef was the artist. I sat down not at the counter but at a table, and I ordered the cheapest item on the menu, a bowl of white navy bean chili, along with a glass of tap water.

I had my back to the women and leaned my blue umbrella against the square edge of the table. It was a tricky lean. I tried three or four times before it caught, balance an elusive force on this day. When the food came, I savored it. Thick enough to eat with a fork—only after several mouthfuls came upon a big round pebble in it which I bit on hard enough to tickle my enamel but not scratch. I spit out the stone into the flat of my hand, without wiping it clean, and put it on the table. I finished my chili, called over the lady, and told her what I'd found. She said there was no charge for the chili, and to this day, I'm thankful that I chew gently when I eat hot beans. I talked to an attorney (my friend and tenant Pete, who was also one of my teachers at Miami University), and my first thought was that the chef be fired and his or her whole lineage be deported to a foreign land. My second thought was if I'd swallowed the stone, it might have cut a vein in my anus when it passed. My third thought was that I was lucky as hell and might as well go to New York whether I was funded, or not and take my chances.

A final note: I was mistaken about the source of Tink's' name. I knew a man who lived next door to the restaurant, a notable Cincinnati artist, whose father was nicknamed Tink. Word around the neighborhood had me confused. When I told my friend about the pebble, he said, "I don't have a dog in that fight." The remark struck me as typical of the man's humor, but even then, I didn't fully understand. You see, the man's father had that nickname, but the owner of the restaurant had no connection to the man named "Tink" but actually to the owner's pet dog, also named Tink, pictured on the awning next to a highball glass.

2

Lacey #1

WE WENT TO TWO parties together, both in one evening. The first was a fiftieth birthday for a local activist videographer I'll call Sal. Sal's partner, Michael, was one of Cincinnati's most prominent theater directors. Mike was one of my best friends. He acts as a bit of a bookend in this story. Both were friends and fellow collaborators of mine. Each contributed to my education as a writer and performer.

The party for Sal was at the urban Mt. Auburn home of an architect and artist couple. Mt. Auburn was a racially mixed and mixed-income residential area between the hospital district and what could be called ghetto. It was a house surrounded by the green of foliage from trees, bushes, and houseplants. Orange and yellow daylilies were in bloom. The owners were serious gardeners. People filled the kitchen and spilled outside, down some wooden steps into the back patio and beyond onto the driveway.

Lacey didn't know how famous all the local luminaries were. I was forty-three and had long gray hair, on this night covered by a Panama hat. Lacey, twenty-one, wore a bright yellow dress and sandals—her legs were mucho furry. A lithe dancer, slight compared to me, features elfin where mine were wide and generous. Lacey's eyes spoke of depth; their gaze and focus implored seriousness. But her grin was full of whimsy and mystery. Lacey had been raised in the small town of New Richmond. Her mother ran a small Empress Chili-shop ice cream stand on the river highway east of Cincinnati. When I was a teenager, I used to bicycle upriver on the Kentucky side, take the New Richmond ferry, and then cycle home along the Ohio, past River Downs and Coney Island.

We'd met at Sitwell's. I'd been attracted by her posture, the shape of her shoulders and bare biceps, and had struck up a conversation with her, something about theater and poetry. Sitwell's had just moved from its original location two blocks west, under Tudor Court Apartments on Ludlow Avenue. Lisa, the owner, a friend since high school, took over the Cove from Dave who was part of the series of events that evolved my nickname "Citizen." Lisa renamed the place Sitwell's after Edith Sitwell, a British poet from the early 20th century.

One time in the Cove, Neil Aquino, an assistant to a City Councilman heard me complaining about a pothole. He said that he could get it filled if I told him where it was. So, over a period of months, I received official mail from City Hall's Public Works Department about filling potholes. The letters were always addressed "Dear Citizen Lansky." I started Neil with an easy one, and sure enough, it was filled in a matter of days. The second task was to remove a set of railroad tracks on Elsinore that went nowhere. I complained that they were uneven, unused, and were doing damage to the suspension systems of cars. Next time I came around the Cove, Kelly was there hanging out on a barstool, smoking and chatting up Dave. I thanked Neil and kidded with Dave about being called "Citizen." Dave, the barista, and Kelly, his girlfriend called me Citizen from then forward.

Sal asked Lacey some innocent questions, finding out that she was a theater and dance student at Northern Kentucky University. As the crowd grew, we talked with Sal's mother, and she and a small group of other early arrivals doted on Lacey's presence, gentle, sincere, and warm. Later, one of the other women asked me—is she your daughter? Your student?

I said, "She's a daughter and a student." Then with a deep breath and a wry smile, "Not mine."

We escaped the matronly women for indoors where a jazz quartet performed with energy. Lacey sipped wine. I tried to fill up on hors d'oeuvres, gobbling down chicken fingers. As the lawn began to fill up with the artsy crowd I knew from when I was married, I reflexively withdrew and fled, Lacey gracefully stepping along with me.

The second party, at an industrial loft in the David Shoe building, was mid-performance when we arrived. This location, in a mostly black urban ghetto, had a frenetic energy on the street that slipped through the door with us. A blue bulb lit a microphone where poets were rattling away, toking joints, beating congas, angularly attired, in lumps on the floor, steel pillars blocking chairs, sitting pillows scattered around. A haze of smoke, bottles of wine—men with berets and velvet jackets, shouting tension. Shtick pouring out of the poets' young pores. Lacey drifted from me, unmoored as I was, after confessing in an animate whisper, her face close to mine, a strong interest in the fellow with the velvet coat. Ahh—I too had velvet in my past—but now I opted for white linen and silk. I felt nervous—too much party, too much buzz, buzz. Too much style, too much shtick elbowing here and there at others. Thinking remotely of decorative verse, *The New Yorker* and how this whole scene was painted a little rough-edged, a little Cincinnati urban. I had no idea of what was to come, when I would leave this inbred city where I felt shtick was re-invented from shouting to cursing . . . . Yet my peers were here, too, and I felt like I liked them better in the academic setting than in this warehouse ghetto. My community-based roots were turning bourgeois, and I could feel it. My shoes were scuffed, but my heart was scraping.

Lacey's charms were close, but she had already wrenched more of my heart than I ever would of hers. She spun with ecstatic energy. I sat in serenity. She chided me that I was too sedate, not wild enough, not sufficiently kinetic.

3

Lacey #2

I MADE THE DECISION to purchase a train ticket. I won't tell about arriving at a dark passive monolithic Art Deco station that few even know still serves the train traveler. Built as train travel declined, this landmark never achieved full utilization; it had basically been a museum for over a decade now. The mosaic tile murals above the rotunda depicted, on a grand scale, pioneers and Indians facing industrial captains in sharp suits and ties.

After midnight, wandering underneath the cavernous dome, I found the chains down across the Amtrak counter, so I pushed open a series of doors out to the platform. Steel clanged behind me. I was locked out. A disembodied voice from an electric megaphone scolded me. I was surrounded by concrete and metal, tracks with cinders, and buried wooden creosote ties. Electricity smelled like diesel. I paused to decide if the air was moist or damp, as a writer might if he were considering going to New York City by federal transit. What if there was an air strike? All the madness of weather in the country had left me stranded in airports a year before. This time I was primed for rail travel.

A man in Sitwell's coffeehouse, Alex, had talked to me about vintage train cars. He was a film director. A compact Brazilian with a devil-may-care grin, a perpetual sweat, a shock of salt and pepper hair, and the fire of a racecar driver, he listened to me spin out script ideas that he might develop. He wanted to do a movie with train travel. Gesturing with small strong hands, speaking with an accent, he poked a finger in my chest, uttering warm, angst-ridden blessings. His afternoon habit was to drink into the evening.

As I stood on the platform, the voice came again. The Brazilian's voice in my head, the disembodied railroad voice of authority, clicked an electronic switch and told me to pull a door handle. I was back in the terminal. A man appeared, then another. They pulled the chain-link barrier up from the counter.

After a long chat with these two laconic men who peered at me over hidden desktops that were their cosmic ties to a secret network, I was able to secure a round-trip Amtrak ticket with my Discover Card. The ticket had train numbers and times and covered a loop that would take me to New York City through Washington, DC, and Philadelphia with a return path north through Cleveland and Chicago, arriving back in Cincinnati in less than a week. Altogether it was a fine document. Who was to know how important that red slip of paper with its carbons and smelly ink would become to me? In these wee morning hours, I debated when and where to sleep. I knew I didn't have time to get a full night before the train departed. I had been the cause of the raising of the chain fence over the ticket counter. Now, would I dare to wait there in the station for hours? No. It occurred to me that I should call my Case Manager and cancel our appointment for the next day, let him know I was going away. He always came to my house promptly on schedule. He trusted me. It was true that I'd mentioned the possibility last week of going on this trip, and I could certainly leave him a voice mail. But for some reason, I stood at the payphone, thinking, No, I'll call him when I get back.

I walked out into the night then through the concourse with the mosaic tile above, the dome looking regal as though the thirties were yesterday, as if Spain had just come out against Franco and Mussolini, as if no one knew that a slumbering Ohio was waiting for me to come to my senses and say good-bye to the big green fountain a few miles away. The heart of downtown Cincinnati was the Tyler Davidson Fountain, designed and built by Greek immigrants, it anchored a town that was provincial in its hilly urban and suburban neighborhoods. Over forty feet tall, topped by a sculpted woman, water spraying from her outstretched hands to tiered platforms, complete with nymphs and cherubs, the woman called by some, the Genius of the Water, presided over the square. She'd been moved and turned more than once, now she greeted the Western visitor, where once she faced the East.

My Toyota had a yellow daisy in a Stewart's Orange Creamsicle bottle in the drink holder, reminder of a second amusing date I'd had with Lacey, nearly a week before. Somehow the flower had lasted!

A friend had gifted me two tickets to Rusalka, the opera at CCM, and I thought to myself, You're reinventing your social life, so just ask her, do it, why not?

She said, Sure, told me to pick her up out in New Richmond at her mother's Empress Chili. Man, was that all there was to it? Why didn't I do this all the time?

Two nights later, I found my way to New Richmond, driving out Highway 52 as the sun set behind me. Lacey wore a simple green dress that revealed the curve of her small breasts. Her eyebrows danced when she spoke. When she looked at me with those pale blue eyes, I felt a charge of excitement that stirred in me a recollection of a girl from my teen years who had not requited my advances.

We saw *Rusalka*, in Czech, translated by Kvapil (or was he the librettist?) on the campus of the University of Cincinnati. I think the two of us radically lowered the demographics of the audience, both in age and income. During intermission, we talked nonstop. Lacey seemed calm, preternaturally serene for her age. I guessed her theater studies at NKU had imbued her with confidence. Her mother, I learned, ran a camp in the Florida Keys. Her dad liked to fish and go boating in the Mangrove Keys.

Somehow, we got onto the topic of hallucinogenic experiences, and that led to a discussion of our time in rehab. As the curtain came up on the second and final act, we engaged in a friendly dispute over the origin of the word "homogeneity." I was being rather loud and adamant, and a stuffy English professor type hissed at me to be quiet. Lacey, lips pursed, turned and razzed him—a loud lip-thrumming blatty raspberry. That one moment alone endeared her to me, and the feeling only blossomed as we walked across Nippert Stadium's fake grass field after the final curtain, she barefoot, sandals in hand, smoking a cigarette. We bumped knees and shoulders once, twice, three times, as we walked, the tease of the bumping somehow affecting the tone of our voices as we talked about the Mermaid. A musky scent partly masked by her cigarette hovered in the cool night. Her pink painted toes in the fake green grass looked pale, translucent under the lights. We were part of humanity, and we were human, and I felt pride. This could last a minute, an hour, a day, or a month. Her shoulder, lower than mine, showed bare, the strap of her dress there, and a gray sweater dropped onto her bicep, seductive, tenuous.

I drove her back to Ludlow Avenue, down the street from Sitwell's, where she met a friend with whom she would spend the rest of the evening. When I ducked down to kiss her goodnight, our faces were not centered on one another, and so my lips caught part face and part moist, half-open smooch. No matter. She plucked a daisy from the window box outside Habañero's and gave it to me, and when I got back to my car, I placed it in the Stewart's bottle.

Now I drove through the night-dampened Cincinnati, found a parking spot, and hiked over the uneven curbstone in heavy iron-toed shoes. At the downtown Fountain Square, water sprayed over my long gray, uneven, and flowing hair, sprinkling on my round glasses and catching in my black beard. I knew I would be away for almost a week and I wanted to ask Lacey out one more time before I left. Meanwhile, I mused over my coming adventure, advancing a plot for train rides. Would all my fellow passengers be going for the same reason I was? Would each of us be heading into our destiny? Why was I choosing to go to The New Yorker Festival at this moment in time?

I'd read an article about dream research in *The New Yorker* when I was in junior high school. My father, a research psychologist, taught a graduate seminar on REM sleep from our living room. One day, when I was home from school sick, Dad let me sit in on the class. While his students pored over Electrooculograms, Electrocardiograms, and EKGs, deciphering the wobbly lines, I wrote a paper for school about dream research that drew on Dad's class and *The New Yorker* article. Ah, *The New Yorker*! It was also where I'd discovered and fallen in love with Donald Barthelme's short stories (Dad called them confused, but I maintained they were carefully constructed for effect). Later, at Harvard, I'd studied with John Batki, a Hungarian writer, who'd published a short story in *The New Yorker*. The iconic magazine had become for me (and for far too many others by my lights) the holy grail.

Off the Haldol, though, my confidence knew no bounds. I felt and believed I knew as much as my professors about poetry. Even so, when I told Keith Tuma, the poet on my committee, that I wanted to go to the festival, he was not supportive. Dr. Tuma had worked closely with me on experimental poetics, but he couldn't have cared less about The New Yorker Festival. Nor could Jim Reiss, the great poet on the faculty at Miami, who had published in *The New Yorker*, but had no time for me or my poetry. Pete Orner, who taught a fiction workshop, loved my novel-in-progress, but he too was skeptical of the trip. Perhaps he had an inkling of what was going on. His girlfriend's brother suffered from schizophrenia. Pete said, "Steve, your mental illness just means you have to be aware of your limitations."

I tried asking Dr. Tuma if he would go with me or consider helping me get some funding from Dr. Brinkman, the Department Chair, but Dr. Brinkman wouldn't return my calls. Did she too, suspect I was unstable?

Frustrated by the lack of support, I grew stubborn, certain that I knew the correct path, angry that no one else seemed to understand. The timing seemed perfect to me. I was 43, finishing a graduate degree. The New Yorker Festival beckoned me. It was my time.

Haldol had kept me predictable. Slow, easy to monitor, and outguess. On Geodon, I could dazzle. Blaze and lead. Show these backwater hicks the way! Hell, I might even be able to teach those New York stars a thing or two.

I was with my mother in my parents' apartment overlooking the Ohio River, listening to a radio discussion of T.S. Eliot's *Four Quartets*. Distress swept her face as I pontificated grandly. My studies in English Literature had reached a level beyond her understanding. I had read more widely and deeply than she ever had. She had struggled for years to pass the Professional Psychology Licensing Exam. Now, as I explained Faulkner and Eliot to her, she admitted that she had never been able to comprehend Faulkner, didn't have the background to understand. The radio host on the NPR affiliate at Xavier University discussing Eliot was someone I knew. We had competed for listeners when I worked at Northern Kentucky University's NPR affiliate. Now the whole thing made complete sense to me. I needed to go find my equals and they were in New York City. Twenty years earlier, I had written a piece that Roger Angell had rejected with a personal note. He said my work appeared too familiar for avant-garde writing. Here, in Cincinnati, the consensus among my parents' friends and colleagues was that my work was *too* avant-garde. I was faced with this hopeless divide, understood that even in the global community, no Cincinnati writer could be taken seriously unless he physically traveled to New York, to the literary center of the universe. If the English Department faculty at Miami were against my going, or worse, indifferent, maybe that was all the more reason to go!

The water shifted from the internal flow to the external. I'm not sure how it works, but there was a diagram somewhere. I let my mind become empty, and my eyes followed the streams as they sometimes leaped and other times grew, guided by a hand of man? Or water pump? And were water pumps gravity-driven? I felt my pulse in my temple, the moisture on my skin, saw light in the translucence of a dream.

Night both dark and gleaming like a pistol under the moon, or a rifle with a mother-of-pearl inlay on obsidian, a flash of time enhanced by lack of rest. Cincinnati had been under siege. Police sirens were quiet tonight, but I had heard that Federal Investigators were moving in to control the population. The Feds would monitor the Cincinnati Police. My relations with protesters and police had become unworkable.

The day before, after the incident at Tink's, I had trumpeted my concerns to my colleague and friend Pete, who was a lawyer as well as a teacher. Pete was compact, had a clear voice, a full head of brown hair, sharp blue eyes, a jaw that jutted a bit when he spoke, and a tendency to sound a bit whiney when he complained. He was a brilliant writer and teacher, who had studied under André Dubus. Although he advised me not to go to New York, Pete still gave me information about hostels to stay in there.

The Thursday (or was it Wednesday?) before I left, I had taken my Madrid guitar to the coffeehouse to air it out, play a song and stretch out. While I had the instrument, a fine mahogany classical gut string, on the side of the window seat, a very dark-skinned black man named Sam, whom I knew from various street encounters over the course of the years, began an odd series of movements outside the storefront window on Ludlow Avenue. Sam had a wide flat nose, and the darkness of his skin made his teeth and the whites of his eyes blaze. He wore a dark, helmet-shaped hat, and equally dark clothes. I couldn't hear anything but his curses, but it looked to me as if he was protecting or fighting a demon that no one else could see. I'd first encountered him seven years before and had watched him move around the community. He did not belong in this kind of civilization. Kung Fu Sam was a man out of time. For some reason, I became convinced that he was protecting my guitar with his sidewalk gyrations, distracting attention from the value and beauty in my hands—the instrument I was prevented from playing by all the pain inside. I meditated on a mantra while he danced to a rhythm that only he could hear. I counted his steps, watched where he hitched to the left, flailed his arms, and gestured up and down, his finger moving quicker than I could follow. As he moved and picked up energy, he paused, gathered himself, and then parried forward seven to fourteen counts, though I could not see his feet. Perhaps he'd have made a pretty good fencer, in a time when fencing mattered. Today, he would be arrested.

As he danced off the sidewalk into the bus stop where waiting commuters moved aside to accommodate his rhythm, three police cars arrived and spilled out two men and one woman. The three cops triangulated in their blue pants and starch white shirts, with their hats perfectly in place, pistols on belts, steady hands calming. Sam let them cuff him and then pleaded something in a voice I couldn't hear. I imagined he said that there is a Madrid guitar inside that coffee shop that is waiting to be touched and needs protection, and I am guarding it.

Returning to the deep night Art Deco train station with its mosaic scenes of pioneer days, I left the daisy in the Stewart's bottle in my car unprotected. The train left on time, with many passengers, arching with aching timeless music that had no refrain into a wet morning along the Southern banks of the Ohio River.

It may help to know that I'm protected for a little while, more each day, but there are these periods when I have to test the men and women who work all day and all night to see these kinds of pictures. The two-day period before I left Cincinnati for New York City was one of viewing and leading. After Kung Fu Sam came up, was arrested, and disappeared, Pete the teacher, and I got caught up in a little wrangle. Looking back, I think I believed that Pete also knew of Kung Fu Sam's arrest and, in his role as a lawyer, became involved. Maybe this was the beginning of the loss of my mental stability. Pete might well have been helping Kung Fu Sam with his legal problems, but there was no such doubt as to my becoming concerned over the plight of these marginal black men of my generation who begged in the neighborhood.

I had another friend, Frank, who had been a fellow social worker in days past, as well as a lawyer. Frank was round and bulbous, his voice mushy and often slurring. He walked with a limp, shirttail nearly always untucked, though he often put effort into replacing it when he stood up from his desk. His features were nondescript, and he worried that he would never amount to much. In fact, he had compassion for his clients out of proportion to the expectations of his supervisor, so he was often defending random acts of kindness. Kung Fu Sam had been one of Frank's social work clients, and because Sam was always getting arrested for jaywalking, my friend Frank intervened with a judge at one point. Frank argued that Kung Fu Sam was a crack addict and needed treatment, not jail time. Somehow these two friends got jumbled up in my mind with the case of Sam. I think I was just so disturbed by seeing this arrest that I began to get confused.

What can be tracked through this chapter, from the train to the Mermaid, the lake not mentioned, the light so special, with Lacey and the fountain on separate summer nights, is that I was a lonely man on the verge of losing his mind. Kung Fu Sam was likely in a jail cell or somewhere riding a bus. His focus, longer gone than mine, still affected me as I was losing focus rather gradually and in a harmlessly charming way, I hoped.

I have so much to say, and I would like to get back to detailing the train journey from the Union Terminal on the CSX limited, but I dare not describe how I came to know that the train would be the best way to avoid access. Maybe I should come out and say it? I'd been thinking and chatting at the coffeehouse about making films and may have imagined that now, with the train adventure to come, I was actually in a film. The director fellow with whom I'd dialogued, Alex, had suggested trains for atmosphere. "Write a film that takes place on a train," he'd said.

And so, in my mind, I had.

4

WAILING WHEELS

THE WAILING OF THE steel wheels along the edge of the tracks kept me attentive to the curving path over the Ohio River. The first hour moved by slowly, just as the train was slow leaving the city on the northern bank. At dawn, we reached Maysville, Kentucky, cruising along next to Route 8 between the narrow highway and the wide muddy. School children disembarked at Maysville, obviously part of a tour. Their chatter was warm, they took flash pictures, and the teachers and parents with them grinned, as all were well behaved.

I remembered cycling on Route 8 as a teenager, racing freight trains on these tracks. A small group of us had ridden to Maysville once in the seventies and had our picture on the front page of the local newspaper. The passenger cars were comfortable with wide upholstered seats, good lighting to read by, and an observation car; its windows curved above the pastel-colored, cushioned, rotating chairs to allow a view of trees and sky, as well as the farm buildings along the way.

Lacey needed me to be a man of action. I wanted her to read about me. I wanted her to know I could take charge. As I felt the train move beneath me, my gut tightened with desire and discomfort. Was it hunger or a need for something different? A young woman might satisfy me. She would miss me. At least, I hoped she would miss me. I could see her face when I closed my eyes. When I opened them, the world blew past the reflective windows twisted like the black limbs of trees in gray mist. Faces appeared to me—distillate and abstract. The sounds of the train, unsettling at first, came to provide a rhythm to my longing.

5

Lacey #3

"MY MONOLOGUE," SHE SIGHED.

"I'd love to hear it," I said.

"The teacher didn't like it."

I wanted to ask her why but thought better. She was starting to climb down the inside of the long-necked brown beer bottle. I was hoping her experimentation would lead to insight. I don't remember how we got to it, but when we were talking about cars, driving, her '86, blue, Toyota pick-up truck, and insurance, she let slip she'd had a bit of trouble with the local constabulary out in New Richmond, where she lived with her parents. I wondered right away if there was a D.U.I. We'd had the conversation about romance, and she'd insisted she didn't see me as a romantic partner yet, though there were hints of something, a hug, a look, a kiss blown through the air. Still not enough.

"You're too slow, Steve, too sedate. I'm looking for excitement."

I understood. I was large and moved with a deliberate sense. But I didn't want to scare her. She had her dancer's lithe body, a kinetic sense that drew me into her with motion. Nabokov's Humbert called Lolita Lolly, Lo, or Dolores, depending on the time of day. Lacey hugged me, looped long arms about my shoulders lacelike, but when she moved, she was an Ace. Her cleverness became a game of Acey Deucy, gambling with my affections. Her other friends were young dancers. I had not seen her dance with others, but in the coffeehouse after closing time, while she guzzled beer, her feet spun while her long arms and hands waved up and down, held almost perfectly out to her sides. Her head moved cobra-like on her long thin neck, chin level, never high in pride, nor bowed in modesty; she danced like an old, old memory to me. An electric gaze kept me in focus, and a toothy white smile edged from behind tempting pink lips. I wanted to reverse the polarity. I had danced with an older girl when I was a young man. Now I wanted to dance with this young girl. Watching her move, I felt a sober stirring down below and wanted more. I stepped outside to the bench on the night street.

She played her part proudly but sloppily, swinging the longneck brown beer bottle in her hand, stepping off the curb and shouting at the flashing night street, performing her monologue about a suicidal moment, voice rising in the moonlight. Her voice modulated as she tried to use a southern accent before retreating into her own voice, spinning out into acted anger. I felt that she was inexperienced and that she was looking to me for answers that could only be found within. Still, I wanted to coach her, help her stay with her voice and not feel a need to pretend. I could see a retained flicker of anger in her eyes as she stood there, shyly, thin legs apart, waiting for me to say something.

"My teacher gave me a D for this monologue," she said at last as I stayed silent. She drained her beer and tossed the bottle into the can on the sidewalk. A man had come out of Sitwell's Coffeehouse and was locking up. It was Caleb, a curly redheaded folk guitarist. He was clearly drunk. I asked him if I could borrow his standard one-speed bicycle for a few minutes. He said, "Sure." Lacey looked up at me with her elfin face shining in the streetlights. On this cool spring night, the moon rose high over the streetscape.

"Sit on the handlebar," I said.

She propped her thin behind up onto the chrome bar, let her arms dangle. "Place your insteps on the axle nuts on either side of the front wheel," I said.

I stood on the pedals, and off we went, moving gently, rocking and swaying down the sidewalk under the marquee of the Esquire Theater, which had a light out so it read, SQUIRE THEATER. Lacey laughed a bit, not at all nervous, and then squealed with pleasure as we bounced past the Mediterranean Store and Biagio's Bistro. As we approached the flower shop,

I warned her I was going out into the street. She leaned into my arms. Our heads were side by side, and her long brown hair blew across my eyes. We canted a bit as we edged off the curb on the handicap ramp at the corner. The traffic lights clicked and buzzed, but there were no cars coming from any direction. I spun us out into Ludlow Avenue past the Firehouse on the corner facing the flower shop. We swung in a half-circle, and I pumped my legs easily, picking up speed coming back toward Sitwell's. Our ride was short and spirited, just one block each way, but it was enough to give me a glow. When I steered us onto Telford Avenue in front of the ice cream shop, Lacey turned her head and grinned, her face full and happy. I wanted to kiss her as we stopped, but I wasn't that forward. Her hair lay on my hands while I stepped down from the pedals. She dismounted, laughing. My heart was thumping. My breath came quickly.

The sky grew gray, and the rain fell as the train passed coal cars filled and waiting to go to the cities of the north and east. The muted colors of the green trees with their dark trunks, the golden and green fields, the earthy water, the glow that seemed best under a light rain and a gray-blue sky in the earliest morning; these were the shimmering farms of rural Northern Kentucky. Barely in the South, the river had a soothing, powerful presence as grandfather wisdom surfaced in my mind in little sayings that I wish I had written down. Cincinnati behind, a great adventure underway, I began to meet some of my traveling companions.

There was an architect in the observation car who worked in Covington. He was something of a cyclist as well. We talked about carpentry and construction. His presence was good and mellow, and we seemed to be politically okay. The only black people I saw were workers on the train. The architect's name was John, and he had deep-set brown eyes, shaggy brown hair, and a full mustache. He was interested in my plan to go to the New Yorker Festival in Manhattan. He was traveling alone, headed for Baltimore for a holiday with family.

When the call on the overhead PA system came for breakfast, I was hungry and eager. In the dining car, the Amtrak family served, and the rule was four to a table, no matter the size of the party. So I met and mingled with a man who worked on mainframes using UNIX, his wife, and their traveling companion. The man was fifty-three, balding and conservative.

He wore a golf shirt, and when he got up, I saw and had my suspicion confirmed that he had tassels on his shoes.

As the train clicked along towards West Virginia, the man's wife and their traveling companion blended into the background, nearly disappearing. I thought about H.G. Well's novel, *The Invisible Man*, and how invisibility was a result of solubility. As they became saturated with liquid (like a piece of paper soaked in oil becomes translucent), they appeared to be part of the interior of the train. Likely interiors and upholstery, bulkheads, and floor tiles were their natural surroundings, a kind of habitat for them that exempted them from any individuality, allowing them to be virtually non-existent to all but the keenest observers. I was privileged to have the ability to observe all of this, but as I let my imagination flow freely, I wanted to comment to the threesome on the twosome's humble lack of individuality. I wanted to say, "Existence is a struggle, and unless you put your shoulder to the wheel of identity, you may never be counted." As I grew more vested in my sense of self, I failed to foresee the need to keep my head down, which was coming my way faster with each click of the large train's wheels.

I was still pondering the fate of Kung Fu Sam. There had been articles in the local press, Federal Investigators on the scene checking up on our police force. Race riots, civil unrest. Boarding the train, I'd noticed several black families chattering loudly outside the gate. But since departing, I hadn't seen them again. It was as if they were on a different train.

I returned to my seat after breakfast, looked out the window, read a bit of a *New Yorker* story by Salman Rushdie that reminded me of myself—since I was wearing the same Panama hat and the white clothes he described. The coincidence elicited strange feelings of kinship and ratification, but also paranoia, the idea that something had been taken or stolen from me. But still, I felt justified in having decided to get out of Cincinnati. I was headed for the center of all centers, where I would be recognized at last. Maybe I would be able to meet an editor and talk about the publication of my poem, *Gogol's Ear.* Surely it would not be for lack of my effort. I would no longer disappear into the slush pile of poems that rolled over the transom through the rejecter and back into the U.S. Postal Service bag in the S.A.S.E.

As the train began to roll into deep hill country along the New River, lunch was announced. This time, I sat across from a short woman with curly blondish hair piled haphazardly on top of her head. She ventured a reluctant grin that revealed a badly capped front tooth, which, combined with her Southern accent, suggested a certain weakness of breeding. I say this because her short stature, grayish complexion, and downcast eyes gave her away as a smoker and drinker, and though I can't speak to the science of it, I think my experience as a licensed counselor qualifies me to make such judgments.

Her husband, for his part, had a shock of white hair, a paunchy gut under a navy golf shirt, and a flinty look in his eye. He sat tall, with a bold jaw, and appeared reluctant to have me join them at their table. When I asked him what he did, he replied tersely, "Retired from the Air Force."

"What rank?"

"Major."

"Did you serve in Vietnam?"

"Three tours," he said with matter-of-fact pride.

"Ever read *Catch 22*?"

"Uh-huh."

"Major Major?"

He was silent for a moment.

"I'm betting you were a major fuck-up." I'm not sure what prompted me to attack him in this way, but the words came out quickly before I could stop them.

"I don't have to take that from you," he said. "Either you're mighty weird, or you're on drugs."

"I'm twelve years straight and sober, a chemical dependency counselor, but I am one of the weirdest people you'll ever meet. Want to buy some drugs?"

"Get away from us, you weirdo." He turned to his wife. "Come on, honey, we don't have to put up with this." He leaned toward me, appearing to want to get in my face, but seeing how much bigger I was, he changed his mind, taking his wife by the arm. Size did matter, apparently.

"I have Naproxen Sodium for sale," I continued undaunted. To his wife, I said, "I can refer you to a dental surgeon who can help with that tooth."

She hissed, "Well, I never," under her breath as he ushered her to another table.

He'd looked so smug as he uttered the word "Major," I'd wanted to punch him in the face. Just weeks earlier, I'd reread Catch 22, and fresh from the story, his self-importance irked me.

Still, I'd like to say that I knew I had gone too far, that my happiness at treating him and his wife so rudely had hurt my heart. I do not think of myself as a mean person, and it scares me now, remembering how quickly I could turn, how that side of myself could bubble up as if I had a streak of evil right beneath the surface. I know now that it was my schizophrenia that unleashed these demons. Yet I was blind to it as it was happening. Completely and maddeningly oblivious.

A young fellow with shoulder-length hair shaved close on the sides and in back entered the dining car a few minutes after the Major and his wife fled and sat across from me. He was reading a hardback novel and listening to a Walkman, which he took off hospitably so he could make conversation. The novel, he told me, was a gift from his girlfriend who flipped burgers at Burger King. He let me leaf through it. It was a sort of heavy metal romance novel. It was clear the guy missed his girl already.

After lunch, I went and sat in the observation car, and half-dozed through a series of incredible vistas along the New River, one of the few rivers in North America that flowed south to north. We saw Hawk's Nest, some flooded areas, a remarkable bridge, and rolled up and down some great mountain rails into Charleston, West Virginia, where I got off the train with my racing bicycle.

The rain had stopped but would start again before my day ended. The road quickly became narrow and steep. Mud run-off and visible effluvia cascaded along the gutter, spilling brown water and pea gravel across the road. My tires were thin with little tread. I slowed down so much from the grade that I began to lose balance and wobble wide sweeping curves across the roadway. Turning to stay out of the muddy streaming puddles became impossible, and I was barely making progress up the hill. The rear wheel swept out from under me as I ripped my left foot free of the clip-on pedal and caught myself on the slippery roadway. The plastic cleat of my shoe slid, and I was on my ass. Unscarred, out of breath but wet and muddy, I regrouped quickly.

I had started on too steep a path. Head down, I took a
long drink from my water bottle. I turned and went in the
other direction. The road snaked up and down. Soon, I crossed
railroad tracks and paced along through a quiet neighborhood.
Then I came to a wider road. A crossroads. I took it. Soon I was
pedaling among speeding trucks. Grateful that I had worn my
helmet and carried two bottles, I settled into steady pedaling up
and down long grades. I could hear the whine and roar of logging
trucks as they came from behind me. When they passed, gritty
water streamed over me. My greatest fear was that a truck would
come from in front as a logging truck came to pass from behind.
I might be forced onto the gravel shoulder. I smelled the diesel,
the pines, the wet roadway, and my own body.

As I entered the outskirts of a city I came upon John, the
Italian on the green machine. I pulled up on him as it began to
pour rain again. He was more upright than I was, and he was
spinning slowly, pedaling in pain. I didn't know his name, or that
he was Italian, except that was the way it was in the dream, and
here on the train, I knew him as "John the architect who was a
few years older than me." I took a healthy draw from my water
bottle, chewing on grit as I closed it, pushing with my front teeth.

A bike race. Three main competitors coming into Charleston,
West Virginia, from the mountains. Final stage of a big American
race. John and I came upon the cocky young Indian, his head
shaved on the sides. He rode on the Cannondale with the
oversize tubing. We pulled right up to him and kept working
together. I'd had lunch with him on the train. Three together,
one, a young cocky Indian, one, our hero, and the third, an
Italian older lightweight. John and I left the Indian quickly. He
was spent. I knew I couldn't win the race. The oldest won after
the young dropped. The oldest bridged on the flat and then
pulled away in the rain. But we were virtually together, and
emotionally it helped to watch him pedal a little faster. Wait. We
hadn't come to the finish. We pedaled through a set of traffic
lights, past islands separating lanes, and John was confused
about the course. He slowed to look back. I swept past him to
the roar of the imaginary crowd, in the imaginary victory, in the
imaginary bike race.

I woke up with tears streaming down my cheeks. I didn't
dry them but wept openly for several minutes, removing my

glasses, watching the window-blurred rain, as the train pulled into Charleston.

6

LΛCeY #4

I WAS AFRAID TO read *Lolita* because I wanted her to be mine. Sure, she was over twenty-one, but her features, her presence, were young, curvy, thin, silky, girl waif that she was. She taught me the lingo of AOL instant messenger and razzed me endlessly. I tracked her with an angular heart. Humorous inspiration. I left Cincinnati for New York on the train to escape her. How to research the energy needs of a young girl who might date an old fart. We improvised theater in the closing coffeehouse. Sat side by side in the only wooden chairs that weren't upside down, put away on tabletops, our forearms brushing. Titillation, tickle, tease as she read her dialogue from a yellow-lined tablet. My role was all-extemporaneous; I felt that I impressed her in the drunkenness of my affection and lack of Haldol sedation. She eased into a moment of squealing laughter, "Aliens?"

"Yes, aliens with blue eyeliner, pink and black hair, and a desire for peanut butter shakes."

"Beer."

"Beer for a bear in the bar?"

I pulled out a worn Hohner C and puffed my cheeks, pursed my lips, and wailed out a vibe, then a run, a blues tremolo, great vibrato, pause.

"More Lansky, more."

"Lace, what does the light girl say to the dark man?"

"Up and down the scale, dark man. Blow blues that hurt to hear."

She had improvised a line. I blew blue dark and seething, drew lust over the twisted reeds, splitting two holes, and tweaking.

"Yeah, baby," she sang. Her pink lips parted, clean lush white teeth close to my ear.

The harp cradled in both hands wavered, waxed explicit, waned personal; her eyes were on my hands as she reached into her purse, yanked out the ubiquitous red packet and tapped out a single filtered cigarette. I paused from harping, found the pink lighter on the table, flicked a flame to the end of the cigarette that wiggled between her lips, watching the ember grow.

"Ya know the thing is, ya, ya," she rambled.

"I know, ya know, like I say, it's like the thing, ya know, like I said, man, well, like I feel the pain and let it into like, my, like, expression, like, ya know, man?"

"That's when the alien picked up the hammer and found a rhythm," she tapped her fingers on the arm of the chair. "It's a rhythm of the saints, my love."

I melted inside, warm and fuzzy.

"And they came with the night, left their branding irons on the spaceship."

"Did you come alone?"

"Ahh," she said, a grin around the filter, smoke curling around squinting eyes. "But beware the dreaded anal probe!"

We laughed together.

"You have heard the rumors of the dreaded anal probe?" I played along. Did she know of hemorrhoids? Was this a synchronicity? Ahh, sweet pain, longing pangs of humor, and deep dark anguish. Could this be love?

7

Don't Wear Sandals #5 The Film

On Saturday, I walked and rode the subway down to Greenwich Village and walked all the way back. My twenty-year-old hiking boots were falling apart from extensive use. Perhaps it had been a mistake to wear such heavy shoes for a city trip. I began looking for a sandal shop to get some real leather sandals. For years I'd resisted sandals because of the line in that Bob Dylan song, "don't wear sandals, the pump don't work cause the vandals took the handle." But before heading for MacDougal and Bleecker, which is where I was directed by the concierge, I had all my laundry done by the hotel service and lost my clip-on sunglasses and kept calling down to the front desk, asking for different things and getting different voices. Because they were filming a movie in the lobby of the hotel that weekend, I figured it was all a screen test for me, and that the desk clerk was a comedian doing different accents. In fact, I was a bit confused, overwhelmed, and awash in the city that never sleeps. I had been taken in by the beauty and splendor of my credit card.

When I found the subway, I bought a three-day pass for seventeen dollars, which I only used one time. As I got on the train, the conductor in sunglasses, work boots, and with a loud voice, shouted at me that I was getting on the wrong train. At first, I was confused because I hadn't told him where I was going. But he seemed to know something I didn't, even though

I told him I'd read the map on the station wall. Stubbornly, I disregarded his counsel and got on the train, but when we pulled into the Prince Street station, there were workers everywhere laying tile and cutting concrete.

Through the window of the screeching train, I saw the dusty blue-jeaned workmen in heavy leather boots walking around wires. Station after station streaked by, all under construction. The conductor had been correct. And I hadn't listened. When we finally stopped, I got off and walked up to street level with literally no idea where I was.

Teeming masses all around, like a third-world country. I remember corrugated steels shacks, traffic crammed together in lane after lane, as if the street were wide and replaced itself the way sharks' teeth do, in row after row, rolling into place if one were pulled away. There were millions of people bustling around—a throng of street vendors and hawkers and men in all varieties of dress and race.

I stood in the wind shadow of a vendor who was roasting sausages on a stick and decided to buy one and try to take in where I was a little at a time. Then I had another. The sky above was a startling blue, and I was sweating under the straps of my rucksack. I watched a man approach who looked like a native New Yorker. He was bearded, bespectacled, and wearing outdoor safari clothes. A sort of balding cross between Salman Rushdie and the late Allen Ginsberg. I asked him if he would guide me. He said no and told me to just try to conform. I mulled this for what seemed like hours. Try to conform. Try to conform—a rugged mantra.

For a man with a scruffy beard and graying hair in a ponytail halfway down my back, I was radically non-conforming and yet somehow not completely out of place. I walked in Salman Ginsberg's shadow for a block or two and soon found empty streets. I could not believe how people just vanished as I moved. Ten minutes of the crowd, maybe twenty, then the millions of immigrants were left behind, and I was in a trendy area where there were open-air restaurants with painted women, men in tuxes, and crimson roses on every table. The wall murals and artwork of blue and red and yellow and orange filled my gaping view. There were sports cars, German, Italian, Japanese, and cell phones and creases in black trousers, suspenders, bright flowers on jackets, green bottles of wine, mahogany bars, and I wanted to stop, to linger, and I felt invited until I saw tattoos and heavy make-up on a sexy barmaid who leaned provocatively over the bar twisting her leg.

I asked for directions, and her voice was crass and mean. Mean people looked the best. Then I walked past a bicycle rental place where I saw a heavy, shiny, black-framed, three-wheeled rickshaw. By this time, my shoe was coming apart. Strips of leather were peeling out of the inside, and blisters were beginning where the skin was rubbing raw. I asked random strangers for a leather or sandal shop. There was a place run by a fit young Asian man, who offered to glue the leather into place. But the glue would need time to dry, and I couldn't wait. I kept walking.

Now I was thinking about Rushdie's story about the rickshaw wallah and imagined the Chinese man would be the rickshaw wallah if I was casting a film version, and the woman with the tattoos would be the thief's widow. All these attractive people would make a great film. I started scouting locations. Each time I walked in an entryway looking for a leather shop, I smelled leather, looked at boots, belts, and purses, but didn't find sandals, just different shades of heavy leathers, and I noticed mirrors, and entries that part of the view would work for some idea of a film, because there was a film back at the hotel, and to complete it there must be a camera on me.

Writing this now, I know I needed sleep. I was headed for a crash. But I was in New York, in Manhattan, trying to keep up in my Panama hat and white linen blazer and white chinos and heavy, painful boots.

Then somehow, I was out of the crowded gallery, restaurant, shop district and into an area where there was a park with fenced-in basketball and squash courts and a level of exertion in those closed spaces that was impossible to believe. Kinetic movement, frenetic, of all colors, green and reddish pavement, white and black nets, I cannot even recall what the games were or how it seemed other than the sense of being overwhelmed by the sweat and shouting and intensity. I had never seen this America before, this teeming racing activity, shouting itself louder and louder.

Somehow, I found MacDougal Street and saw some women planting flowers. There was a space off the side of a side street where there were pretty petunias around a small tree with black painted little fencing to keep dogs out. I knelt on the sidewalk and prayed for a moment. Then I moved on and asked a man at an outdoor café for directions to a sandal place. I thought for a moment that I could be filming an advertisement of how to find the place . . . stop and speak Deutsche to the ladies planting, say a prayer at a tree, ask a man with a tattooed face reading D. H. Lawrence at a café for directions, then buy a small loaf of warm bread at a bakery kitty-corner from the next light, and duck your head, turn ninety-degrees, and there you are at the sandal place!

I sat down, took off my painful shoes, had my feet measured, fondled, and sketched, then learned I'd have to come back in two days for a fitting—what?—and the whole mission was scratched, wasted, in vain. When would I ever come back?

So I walked out of there, all the way back to the hotel. And on the way, I toured delicatessens and food stores, where wealthy people could get anything they ever wanted to eat. I watched a man giving a comedic walking tour of the area, becoming an object of the tour in the process—my movie continued. I talked to street people. I asked a man who was collecting for the homeless if he had heard of a man who had fourteen wives and over thirty children. (I think I was imagining I would be such a man someday, but this is not rational.) And I went into a Florsheim store to see what they had. Footwear occupied my thoughts like nothing else. I went to a drugstore and bought nail scissors so I could trim my toenails and cut the blistered skin. As I arrived back at the hotel, they were filming around the entrance, and there were full plastic bottles of Poland Spring by the curb, just lying in the street. I ignored them, stoically sticking to my role, the man who doesn't know he's being filmed but really does.

Back at the hotel, I took off the boots, tore out the bits of leather that were impossibly torn, and cleaned my blisters. That night I hardly slept but lay in bed, tossing and turning. When the maid came, I just bowed to her and thanked her, but did not let her in. There was also the thing with the candy. There was a jar of hard candy twists in cellophane. I know I heard them popping and cracking magically. I flipped coins on the bed. In the room was a painting of Napoleon and for a moment, I believed that the waiter with the accent who brought the blue glass Saratoga Water bottles that I sent away for a more auspicious occasion was himself, Napoleon. And I believed I was being recruited for the Bolshoi ballet, and I did many sit-ups and exercises in the room on the floor.

I recognized the variety of rose on the dinner tray, because I had one in my front yard, though it died last fall, or should I say it never came back this spring. The variety is called "Singing in the Rain," and the blossom is a peach, tinged with an edge of blood orange. One characteristic unique to this variety is that different blossoms on a given bush vary in color. My friends Po and Jackie gave me the bush as a wedding present.

I had been so moved by the beauty and scent of the large healthy flower on the tray that I had put it out in the hall on the tray when I was finished, thinking, this is too brief to hold onto, I just want a good sniff. The room service at the Algonquin had been slow, but the food was expensive and savory. I had fruit for one meal, braised chicken for another, and a delightful broiled salmon fillet with perfectly steamed green beans and carrots. Lying on the bed, without getting under the covers, I relaxed, breakfasted, lunched, and dined. I had the credit card, so what matter? The problem was sleeping. The hours dragged.

Can a man have so many delusions? Yes. I had so many then that I cannot believe it, myself. It's kind of a testament to the ability of the mind to twist and turn in thin air. Ever since Tink's where the stone in the soup had touched me, I was aware that I was destined to come to New York City. I heard a Cincinnati adman and radio broadcaster in my head lead me to the Algonquin Hotel. I felt guided by the stars and I would not be disappointed. This was the real deal.

Saturday night I had gone out to the Bob Dylan tribute. I must tell about seeing Tracy Chapman perform. Yes, I must tell. I had left with enough time to walk there but had been afraid to ask for directions. I felt that people in New York were as likely to misdirect me as direct me. Yes, I felt that. So, I hiked at night up and down the streets. I think I hiked on Broadway for a while. I was looking for Town Hall. After being cursed out by some drunks who called me a "high roller" and seemed ready to mug me, I found a yellow taxi.

The driver, a very dark-skinned black man with a shock of gray hair, spoke English with a thick French accent and located the place in a matter of minutes. I drove a hard bargain with a scalper. Since the show had started, he lost his service charge!

I thought I was so street. I sat in the balcony and listened, marveling at the lectures on the poetry of Bob Dylan. The crowd laughed as if they were getting in-jokes that I missed. A great big theater full of people who were fascinated with Dylan. I even cried a little.

At intermission, I moved to the first floor and got a better seat. Tracy Chapman's hair was longer than pictured on her old album covers, and she looked young and beautiful and sang with grace. There were other musicians whom I couldn't identify, a man and a woman, both with made-up faces, but they seemed to hang in the air, and the moment lasted longer than it could have in reality, but I was out of touch with reality.

Afterward, I walked to Times Square and watched it at night for a while before returning to the Algonquin, with the doorman who looked like the man in the New Yorker Magazine and the tiny bright elevator and the twelve flights of stairs that I liked to walk down. And somehow my disorientation in New York carried me through all this.

The next morning, I walked in front of the empty stage in Bryant Park after the outdoor reading of the New Yorker Festival was over. In the lee of the chill wind, at the far side, two of the poet/speaker women stood speaking with a much younger woman in an attractive skirt, with shoulder bobbed sandy hair, clear blue eyes, black leggings, shoes that weren't good for walking, and soft features, very easy on the eyes. One of the women asked what I needed. I said I was just trying to get in the lee of the cloth blowing in the breeze at the back of the stage. There was a murmur of approval, a nod; and the younger woman said they show films on that cloth in the summer. The other two echoed, questioned, and the three circled this idea gently.

At that moment I thought about saying, I'm Steve Lansky and I've come a long way on the train from Cincinnati to hear the poetry, and I have a poem, *Gogol's Ear* that I've sent into *The New Yorker* without a cover letter, and it's been several months and I'm a media representative from *OxMag*, in Oxford, Ohio, at Miami University. But I realized it was too much ground to cover. Still, I wanted to invite all of them to have breakfast with me tomorrow at the Algonquin. I wanted that, but it was more than I could pull out of my depths, and the young woman did a pirouette, her eyes bright and flashing, and I watched the union men pulling cable, and I walked away, letting my white linen jacket blow in the breeze.

8

Leaving NYC on the NJ Train

KEEP YOUR HEAD DOWN, I said to myself.

Penn Station was a nightmare. I sat in a waiting area for the Long Island Railroad trying to read, watching people, and wishing like hell I had brought my laptop computer. This one suit across from me was Abe Fortas. No, not old enough. But I was sure he was working on the case. What case I wasn't sure. But he was on it. He had the briefcase and graying temples and heavy leather brogans.

Somehow I had managed, by using my name, to get the information desk to give me my reservation number—a necessity because the fuckers at the Algonquin hotel had stolen my ticket (along with my clip-ons) and I was sure if I reported the ticket stolen, if I told an officer in the station, I'd end up in jail, arrested, or worse, trapped in a hospital. I knew what happened in places like this. I knew what they did to people like me.

I had a brown paper bag with Rainier cherries to keep me focused. Even so, I was terrified.

Keep your head down.

All the blue chrome escalators and stairs, and flashing lights and electric boards and advertising and shops, and people of all worldly origins. I had a reservation number, but I didn't have my credit card anymore. I'd cut it in half with the Algonquin's scissors right there at the desk, I was so fucking angry. And then, I'd gotten in a cab, hours early, and gone to Penn Station. The cab smelled of grilled kielbasa, onions, sauerkraut, and mustard—yellow mustard—and I was in a yellow cab, but out the window the fragrance, the odor, it wafted, it waved, and it seemed the driver followed that greasy yellow smell. I thought of Chief Inspector Dreyfus, and how Clouseau would follow a smell like that, telling the cabby, "Follow that man with the mustache and the mustard." And in the cartoon, the trenchcoat cinched tight at the waist and the wafting smell lines would come in over the glass of the open car window, into the back seat. And I imagined the smell was the thief, the scent of sausage was the criminal who had stolen my clip-ons and my train ticket. Except now the smell was gone, the trail was cold, and the cab pulled up at Penn Station, leaving me there, bewildered. I hadn't been sleeping much. There was no place to sit. If I fell asleep, I could be robbed.

Keep your head down.

Fluorescent lights, tile floors, wooden seats. I sat for three hours. Or was it two? Or one? Or half an hour? Or twenty minutes? Or just ten? Time dashed and flashed and vanished like the scent of the criminal. Or did it drag like the hand around the clock, ticking once a year?

They announced my train and I thought somewhere I saw a flashing sign, a red-lit display telling me the track number. I walked fast in near panic, trying to conform to the flow, looking for arrows, directions. I was lost. Totally at sea. I saw some Amtrak signs but weren't all the trains out of town going to be commuter trains, not Amtrak to start? I didn't have a clue or a ticket. Oh, what the hell. I got on a train. I found a seat. I kept my head down. A conductor asked me for my ticket and I kept my head down. Down in the cherries, munching, spitting the pits into the brown stained bag, rolling the rim of the bag, muttering and eating and refusing to look up. Different conductors. Gonna throw ya off the train. Then in New Jersey two really big ones, huge, bigger than National League umpires, with uniforms, grizzled faces and hole punchers and change machines, demanding I get off. So I got off at the next stop, onto a drizzly platform in New Jersey. This was some kind of automated station. And all these people were the commuters who traveled this way every day. There were people of all races.

Where did they live? What did they do for jobs? And where was the lock-up for the deviants?

I think I was starting to see where this was going to end. I wanted to sleep. I wanted to sleep but it was drizzling and sitting would dampen my ass, and I was damp in spirit already but did not want to add physical discomfort.

The train I had reserved would have gone north into New York and eventually cut across Pennsylvania on its way to Chicago, crossing northern Ohio and then into Cleveland. It was abundantly clear to me that I was not going to make that train, that I had missed it, and was totally fucked—without a destination or a ticket.

In an unhinged panic, I started shouting at the world that I was a Freddie (The name of the band I played harmonica with in Cincinnati and an acronym for some kind of light on the caboose of a train), thinking that I could get on a caboose, or somehow hop my way out of this jam. I kicked the door of a commuter train and stood there in the darkening afternoon.

Then I did something even dumber. I just randomly got on a commuter train and sat with my head mostly down and watched a girl reading a hardback novel out of the corner of my eye. As she got up to leave, I muttered, "Want to go for coffee sometime?" But she ignored me.

The train emptied. I stayed on. The doors closed, and after a while we started moving slowly until we stopped completely on a siding. I got up and started walking from one car to the next. The sliding exit doors were shut, no way to open them. We weren't at a station. Just stopped for the night on a siding. I was alone. I looked at the dashboard of switches and knobs in the space between cars. The conductor would be able to do something if he were there, but without a key it was hopeless. I tried to open the emergency exit but couldn't. Then I pulled some kind of gasket away from a window and was able to slide it open wide enough for me to fit through. I tossed my pack down, then squeezed out, cutting my finger on the sharp aluminum edge before I dropped down to the tracks below, landing on my hands and knees on cinders. I hiked across the tracks and stood there as it grew dark and misty. I could see overpasses and wires and dark concrete brown-gray walls and lights and creosote rail ties stretching away into the night. I thought of why I had ventured to New York City and why I was here. Several times in my life I'd gone to the tracks and been strangely comforted, but this time I sighed and felt only pain. This was not where I wanted to be.

What happened next is hard for me to tell, I don't understand it. I can't believe it. But it has happened before, and likely will happen again. I stood there, on the tracks waiting. I thought about hiding or walking. But as you may remember my boots were torn up from all the hiking in Manhattan and twenty years of hard use before that. These heavy Vibram sole boots were hurting my blistered, sore, tired, aching, miserable feet. So walking was out. And where would I go anyway? Down the tracks? To the closest station? How far was that? And then what?

As I stood there by the tracks thinking these thoughts, along came a big ole passenger train with light blazing, wheels rumbling, horn sounding loud and long. And it just stopped there, right in front of me. Just stopped.

And—holy motherfucking shit! I had stopped a passenger train in New Jersey! This triumph lasted less than a moment or even a second. Behind me, I heard a motor and saw some lights out of the corner of my eye. A Jeeplike vehicle with lights on top—Amtrak police. Two big ones with bellies and hams for hands got out and approached cautiously, as if afraid of me. They asked my name, put their hands on me, and asked me if I was okay and did I want to step on the tracks and what was I doing out here and was I trying to hurt myself?

I told them only my name. I said I was a federal investigator. And then I said, "Miranda." As they snapped the cuffs on my wrists, they said, "We're not going to hurt you, Steven, we want to help you." I had heard it all before. I knew I wasn't going to jail. I knew where they were taking me, but I was furious because I hated the hospital. How would I get home now?

To these smelly, burly, swarthy men I was just a nut on the tracks, a wacko with fears, to be dumped into the system. They went through my pockets and my wallet for ID and played with their computers and yakked on their radios. They had me, and they were sure keeping me. No train ride home for the literate graduate student who had all but finished his thesis. No access to the great books on his reading list. Instead, I was being given a new lesson in keeping my head down even though I didn't want to keep my head down. Why had I said I was a federal investigator? Maybe because I didn't believe in the current US

Federal Government, and thought that a new revolution was in the air. Big-time eastern feds were invading Cincinnati because of race riots, and I needed to investigate New Jersey.

It doesn't make much sense now that I write it down. But I was overwhelmed, veering toward full-blown paranoia, certain they were trying to control me. All I needed was sleep, medication, to be home, a little help dealing with those stupid fuckers at the Algonquin. Could you get me on the right train, please?

It would be weeks before that would happen. We whisked along a gravel path then up on a freeway, off at a ramp, into a driveway. They walked me into a crisis center of bright lights and sterile smells. Soon I was strapped to a gurney after a questioning session that seemed frighteningly brief, where I again said, "Miranda."

One of the hulking cops said, "He said that before, maybe it's something about his Miranda rights . . .." And then the nurse said, "We'll take care of him," and I prayed, and waited and tried to say something. I don't remember when I started talking, but it was after I was strapped down. I'm not saying what they did was wrong, or right, but it seemed to always happen that way to me. I was a big man and they got worried, and instead of locking me in a cell, they took me to the not-so-normal place. I didn't know where I was. I think they told me then it was Trenton, New Jersey.

I hadn't gotten far, but at least I was out of New York.

9

CRISIS CENTRAL

STRAPPED DOWN, SWEATY, BLOODY finger wrapped in a white handkerchief. Harë Krishna. Krishna Harë. Looking around I was in some sort of crisis center. Rolled, strapped, sitting halfway up on a bed in a room. A private room. Then there was this shaved head dude with lots of piercings and tattoos visible. Do I remember that right?

I cursed at the fucker. Yelled, "I'm an Israeli prisoner, I'm an Israeli prisoner. I know you fuckers want my blood." Chanting Krishna chants. Yellow walls. Black wheels on my bed. Leather cuffs. Humane restraints. Don't struggle. Fluorescent overhead lamps, heavy steel doors. He was sitting outside my door, which was open. Hours passed. Harë Krishna. No doctor. A nurse offered OJ and crackers. Dry mouth. Glad I didn't have to pee. Smelling my sweat. It was hot and I was wearing black gabardines, yellow cotton button-down and heavy boots. Linen and silk Nat Wednesday jacket, very natty. But now I was getting angrier and no sleepier. Eventually, the skinhead guy was gone. Or I was moved, something shifted. Two ugly nurse types came in. One had the needle. I was shouting at every sound I heard. As she came to my feet, I timed a perfect kick and knocked the syringe out of her hand across the room. Panic time. More people. Piercing stars in my vision. A man in a starched white shirt, badge, black boots, big leather belt and shiny buckle. I was sure he was one of the fucking Russians. It was because of Romanova they had me. That was it. He was going to force me into the Bolshoi ballet. I didn't mind, but on my timetable, with my choice of ballerinas. No, that was a delusion. He was pulling my pockets inside out. I was holding my money and keys in my right hand as he yanked off my black belt with the burnished silver buckle. He held me down with his ham hands. He was unshaved, stinky, bad breath, sweaty, pungent. I struggled and they injected me right through the gabardines into my thigh. Fuckers.

I woke up walking into a lobby, holding up my loose trousers while they took my pack and money and keys and gave me back my clothes and my two books and my toothbrush. I was on the ward of a state mental hospital. The Russian cop was gone. Small blessings. I didn't want to ever see or smell him again.

10

Trenton State Hospital

When I think of Trenton State Hospital I think of Craig. Also, the guy whose name I can't remember. The rude bigot. Of course, he was mentally ill. We all were; they didn't make mistakes. Hiram was a former minor league baseball player, thick glasses, bad teeth, huge swollen lips, who liked to talk about his young, permanently decamped wife. There was the hilarious gay black guy who lent me toothpaste after mine was stolen. He claimed to have been in Trenton State twelve times. One story he told, confirmed by the friendlier female staff, was that during an earlier admission, he contacted the coroner's office from the ward, reported his own death, and then laughed up a storm when men came with a body bag to take him away.

I was in a dormitory-style room with five other beds. My bed was closest to the toilet. This meant that in the middle of the night when others would leave the water running, or the light on, my sleep was interrupted. It also meant thieves passed by my wardrobe. There were six plywood wardrobes, and the beds had drawers underneath the mattresses. Of course, it held some convenience for me, too. If I had to pee in the middle of the night, I was right there. The floor was tile, and although it was cleaned twice a day by the custodial staff, it was always gritty. Especially when the weather was rainy. The outdoor areas where we recreated and smoked were not all paved. I didn't smoke, but I liked to observe the smokers, especially Craig.

I think Craig had been displaced in time. Similar to Kung Fu Sam, back in Cincinnati in front of the coffeehouse, Craig had very dark skin, was thin as a rail, and looked very fit as he shouted in his public voice. Coming out of the shower he displayed a six-pack that I envied. I think he could have been a town crier in a different world. He paced and walked more than anyone else on the ward. He announced the smoke breaks before they were scheduled and paced and picked up followers. He would repeat the cry of, "Smoke time, smoke break," sometimes starting ten or fifteen minutes before the scheduled time. He never missed a scheduled smoke break and often engaged in a bit of a shouting match with the staff because of his premature announcements. I'm sure this became very annoying for the staff because it happened day after day, every few hours. I would trail outside after the smokers just to be with the trees and smell the summer. It was most pleasant in the early morning when there was dew on the grass. In the evenings there were real prisoners in orange jumpsuits who policed the butts with rakes.

Three West was a long hallway off a lobby area with a nursing station encased in glass or Plexiglas. There was a med-dispensing area with a half door off to one side, a small sunroom where haircuts were given, and an activity room with a spinet, a TV, a radio, art supplies, and tables. The nicest staff member there was a woman I'll call Julia. She was dark-skinned with cornrow braids and a great attitude. She broke the ice with me by complimenting my hair and offering to braid it. I'd always been a sucker for a woman who wanted to play with my hair.

In the main area, there was a silver half-globe on the ceiling which had hidden cameras for security. The day area was right outside the door of the dorm. There was a TV, which played constantly, and an array of tables and chairs, not quite sufficient for everyone to sit at once. On more than one occasion staff members slept there in front of the TV. A little Indian man often sat barefoot on the floor even though there were posted rules against it. Other patients included a white Trenton police officer, who seemed always to get privileges—go figure. He had a burr cut, was big and overweight, and sarcastic. Apparently, he suffered from depression. At first, I was sure he was there to investigate me. He arrived a day or two after me and left a few days before I eventually did. His name was Chris, and behind the tattoos and the puffy cheeks, he turned out to be an okay guy. Chris tried to negotiate a later bedtime for the men during the NBA and NHL playoffs. For the NBA, with Philly in the finals, trash talk filled idle time. The staff could be heard discussing wagers and nightclubs where Iverson was alleged to have been seen. The New Jersey Devils won the Stanley Cup and Chris managed to help a few of us see some great hockey late on Fridays and Saturdays.

Driver, a half-black, half-Puerto Rican staff member who was way into trains, models, history, and current usage, was one of the ones who let us watch. Another staffer, Danny, put on the dog to come to work with his gabardines and gold chains. He also bent some rules for Chris. Danny was a blues guitarist and singer. We talked songs a lot. There was one staffer, Buster, with cornrows and tattoos, who acted the gangster role when he wasn't asleep. He had a mean streak and scared me.

Tom, a young guy, who rapped with vigor and ambition and had a roly-poly body that burst and bulged out of his T-shirt, got into an argument with Buster over who the great rappers were. Tom claimed to have a recording deal, but his story was sketchy and he *was* in the hospital, after all, a fact that Buster and Danny used to taunt him.

Of my fellow patients, the one I liked best was Emmanuel, a dark-skinned fellow with a round shaved head. He was low-key, in his thirties, and had a Ph.D. in biology (his dissertation was about pest control for rice growers) from a Japanese university. A Nigerian by birth, he was having a helluva time with his girlfriend and his career on account of his depression. I loved him as a person because we could talk, and he had some status there somehow. We talked about Lance Armstrong's book, *It's Not About the Bike,* and we shot baskets together outside and sat on a bench watching others in the humid summer heat. Emmanuel gave me a copy of *The Temple of My Familiar* by Alice Walker, which was the only book from the hospital library that measured up to my literary standards. Reading it helped me stay sane.

To her credit, Dr. Nuñez, who looked Japanese or Korean, acquiesced to my wishes and kept me on Geodon. (Reflecting back on this, had she instead switched me back to Haldol, perhaps some unnecessary suffering might later have been avoided.) The one thing she did change was to move the administration of the drug to the morning, after breakfast. It helped me sleep better.

But in the interviews with her, Stu, whose role I never knew, and Betty, the social worker, who seemed frighteningly lacking in competence (a sense later confirmed by all my supports and friends calling long distance from Cincinnati), I felt like I was speaking a foreign language.

For example, I told them I was a graduate student at Miami University in Oxford, Ohio, that I lived in Cincinnati, and that I was a writer. I then, in my light delusion, claimed to be working on Chinese and Japanese imagistic poetry, meditation, and game theory. Eventually, though, I told them I was working on a thesis for a creative writing degree. It was scary to talk about writing autobiographical fiction or memoir involving my schizophrenia while trapped in a state mental hospital nearly a thousand miles from home. I explained that I had a reading list and asked if I could go to the hospital library to see if there were books on my list. But somehow communication with them was slow and difficult.

Once I mentioned that I played harmonica in a band called The Freddies. They asked what the other instruments were. I said there was a bassist, a mandolin player, a dobro player, a guitarist who also sang and played kazoo and harmonica, and a second harmonica—me. None of them had heard of a dobro. They asked me to describe and spell it.

With Stu, a short frizzy-haired character with thick lenses in his late fifties, I had a conversation where he said they had my height listed as six foot seven. I'm six-two. He was so short that he couldn't tell real from imagined height. When I asked them at one point if I could have my belt back, they approved it, but Stu would never get it for me. It wasn't until I asked a friendly technician one morning that I got back the actual belt. This was after at least ten days, and Stu saying, "sure, sure," many times.

I haven't mentioned the women's floor, which was on the other side of the nursing station and similar in size and layout to the men's. The washing machine and dryer were at the end of the women's hallway. All the staff on the women's floor were women. Some of them worked on the men's floor, too. At shower time in the evening, a sheet was hung over the fire door in the hallway to indicate that there were men or women in dishabille. I went to shift my laundry from the washer to the dryer while the women were showering. Seeing the sheet hanging on the doors just didn't register. I got chewed out pretty good and my apologies didn't seem to help. The second time I did it, I got a real dressing down. Somehow, I just wasn't able to stay sensitive to such fundamental issues. The staff woman said, "Don't you have a sister or mother? How about a little self-respect?" I told her I had a mother, but no sister, and I was terribly sorry.

They had these team meetings. There were two teams, blue and green. The green team had a team meeting on Tuesday and the blue team on Thursday. But the week of Memorial Day the meetings were canceled. I was struggling with the idea of how long. How long would I be a patient in this place with the pale green walls, the dark green padded chairs, and the lush grassy enclosures? It soon became clear that the staff was just as happy to be rid of me as keep me. But I did not trust anything or anyone. I had payphone telephone conversations with friends in the hallway opposite the nurses' station. I observed the way things worked out for other patients, and I knew I had to be careful.

The bigoted guy whose name escapes me (I think because I disliked him so much) was calling black staff and patients niggers and the Chinese man with long black hair a Chink, and there were other derogatory slurs that he just pumped out as he stumbled about in an overmedicated state like a drunken fool. He would go to the bathroom at night and leave the water running in the sink and the light on. I would have to get up and turn off the water and the light if I wanted to sleep. The Chinese man, Chang, who didn't talk much, slugged the bigot in the face once.

The bigot was on what they called "one-to-one" the whole time I was there. That meant they assigned a staff member to watch or follow him always. This attention spurred him on. He thrived and shouted and accused. Eventually, they'd escort him to the quiet room, drug him up for a few hours until, groggy and stumbling, he'd come back, bitching and moaning about being persecuted. His case was painful to watch. But the real sad case was Craig.

Craig's team meeting came, and they postponed his release. He had already started planning for a discharge. When the release was postponed, he blew. He just started shouting, "Fuck, fuck, fuck, fuck, fuck, fuck-fuck-fuck, fuck, **FUCK, FUCK, FUCK**." For ten minutes. He was so angry and so continuous with it that they warned him a bunch of times, until he stood there in the hallway in blue shorts and a blue T-shirt, anger steaming and searing out of his lips with the energy of all his nights and days in Trenton State Hospital. They knocked him down, dragged him into the quiet room, restrained him in leather restraints, and injected him full of tranquilizers. After that, he was quiet. And a quiet came over the whole ward until eventually things drifted into a somnambulant echo of Craig's "smoke-time" call and we went outside into the warm weather, trying to decompress.

Maybe as a result of this, I didn't have faith in any plan about my own discharge. I had been told by Betty, the social worker, that there was a plan in place, that it involved a train reservation and aftercare, and that when all my ducks were in a row, T's crossed, i's dotted, I'd be released. But I was too impatient. I told them I had credit cards and money. Couldn't they discharge me to a motel in Trenton until my train was scheduled? Dr. Nuñez said simply, "No."

The worst thing about my stay, the awful secret, was that I needed Metamucil or some other fiber therapy to help with constipation caused by the medication I was taking. I told this to Dr. Nuñez and the nurses numerous times. They offered me Colace, which is a stool softener, but I wasn't interested. I'd heard it had some negative side effects and I couldn't see why they wouldn't give me fiber therapy. The food they served was very starchy and low fiber. By the fourth day, my hemorrhoids were swollen and bleeding as if there were shards of stone in the food that cut me. When I complained to the Chaplain, through her glassy blue eyes and white complexion, she said, "All I can do is help you with your anxiety."

"Yes, but that's precisely the point," I said. "The pain makes me more anxious. Can't you go to the team with me to help talk about fiber therapy?"

"No," she said, "I can't do that." And yet she acknowledged that fiber therapy was something she had heard about.

I saw an attorney who advised me that my court date was two days after my discharge date. He was helpful, assuring me that they would indeed discharge me. The quality control officer walked outside with me and made notes on a form. I mentioned my constipation briefly, not as a complaint but just to let him know. I knew by then that I had to keep it low-key.

The whole key was reading. I could take the meds only when they gave them. Once it was nearly thirty-five hours between doses and I was sure I needed it bad and they were testing me. I called my lawyer friend, Pete, at home. He was the one whose advice I had sought back when the cook at Tink's had started me on my crazy journey with the pebble in the chili. His girlfriend said, "Steve, get a book and read."

In the next five days, I read six books. I was never without a paperback tucked under my wrist. I honestly believe I would have lost it if I hadn't been able to calm my thoughts by diving into these cheap novels. Maybe Pete's girlfriend knew this because her brother had schizophrenia. Whatever it was, I do think in a weird way her advice saved my life.

When I had only a couple of days left before my discharge, a new arrival offered to get me books. He called his family and got me a copy of *Alias Grace* by Margaret Atwood. It was on my list for the degree. A pure victory. I could finish it on the train ride home.

11

INTO STEADY MEDITATIONS

THEY WOKE ME EARLY. I washed my bearded face in the tile bathroom and dressed in my light-yellow, button-down shirt, black gabardines, and beige linen and silk jacket. I followed the final instructions, received my Geodon, my wallet with credit cards, business cards, and I.D.'s, my cash in the money clip, and the extra cash they had given me for the trip and the train ticket. I took a last look at the pale green-walled dormitory with its gritty tile floor. A flash of memory that was eerie as all hell swept through me. Every time I had been asked during treatment if I had "been here" before, I had a sense that I was lying when I said, "no." I think a part of me believed they would catch me in this lie, as they had records, but they never let on. It was a question that always came in a series of questions, and the answers never led to any concrete conclusion on my part, except for the sure knowledge that while I was being questioned the questioner was always weighing the length of my stay and the state of my recovery.

The drug and alcohol counselor had been the least helpful. He had light brown hair that looked unwashed and tattoos on both forearms. I told him I'd been clean and sober over twelve years, and that I missed my local meetings. Nevertheless, he denied my request to attend meetings on the ward, saying they were for current users only, and so he couldn't recommend that for me.

I think I might have made a mistake in asking him if he was a veteran (he was). Maybe it turned him against me. It also made me wonder if there was something in my file about my aversion to the military.

My last morning, I knew that my release was planned but I also knew it could be aborted if I didn't toe the line. I got dressed, grabbed a bagel and juice from the cafeteria, and was escorted to a van by two staffers that I'd never seen before. As the van sped through the morning streets, I opened the envelopes they gave me that had my aftercare instructions and discharge plan. While reading, I scarfed the bagel, then looked out the window of the van trying to figure out where I had been.

We arrived at the train station, still the only part of Trenton, New Jersey I'd really seen other than the interior of the Drake facility. I figured out which ticket and which train I needed without help from the staffers. They seemed impressed that I could read the schedule and that I realized that I couldn't get on the first Washington, DC train, because it was an express commuter train. They hadn't known that themselves.

After I said goodbye to them, I headed upstairs to the platform, and as the realization hit me that I was a free man again, I could actually feel my body change, feel my footsteps become lighter.

The train, when it pulled in, was packed. I had to walk down to the far end of the car before I found an empty seat. For protection and to calm myself, I immediately took out my copy of *Alias Grace* and began to read, realizing as I did, that in the 1970s I had cycled my ten-speed through the very region where the book was set. In places where the story particularly piqued my imagination, I made pencil notations in the margins. For example, one of the psychiatrist character's techniques for opening up the dialogue with the alleged murderess in the novel was to give her a piece of fruit or a vegetable to hold while he questioned her. In one instance he shared an apple, in another a yam. It made me wonder about the relative sizes of the produce, which then got me thinking about the size of the character's hands.

Lacey's hands were small and strong. She had flexible fingers. I imagined them intertwined with mine, pictured us walking together on Ludlow, thought of seeing her again, seeing her eyes under those masterfully expressive eyebrows. Knowing that I was headed home, my thoughts ran wild, and desire flooded my heart.

I tried to re-enter the world of the book after this brief daydream, but my mind kept wandering, making other associations. My brother lived in Vermont and was knowledgeable about produce, gardening, and pest control. He was a statistician who researched methods to develop more successful food growing techniques. Reading about Atwood's teenage girl accused of a horrible crime made me think of my brother's young daughter, my niece, who was years from being a teen. It made me wonder if my brother would find this historical novel as compelling as I did or if he would simply be horrified.

The books I had read during the hospital stay included one about a college professor traveling to India, one about a Greek shipping family (probably the Onassis clan), one about black women in a variety of sexual relationships, one about an Egyptian king and his harem, and a couple of others that were such quick reads that they slipped unnoticed from my memory.

I again went back to reading, but soon looked up again. The young woman next to me had gotten off at the last stop. A Japanese businessman boarded and sat down in her place. The train felt wonderfully modern, full of people who looked nothing like the people I had just lived with the past three weeks.

And yet I felt an odd sense of privilege to have spent those three weeks with them. As a well-educated, middle-class, white schizophrenic, being around that mixture of young and old, black, Asian, African, Puerto Rican and white, the downtrodden and the unique, seemed remarkable and unlikely. It gave me a sense of humility and expansiveness to have shared that time, even if it had not been by choice.

I changed trains in Washington, DC. In the station, I found a pharmacy and got some suppositories for my hemorrhoids along with a fiber supplement. I browsed a bookstore, walked outside, and checked out a fountain on a traffic island. The train station was quite grand, with tile floors, tall pillars, railings, and high ceilings with skylights. On the way to New York, I'd stayed in the waiting area and never seen what the station had to offer.

To my astonishment, the train was the same one I'd taken east. I recognized the porters. Was it a mere coincidence? Soon I settled into an observation car. A man with a khaki multi-pocketed vest was doing a crossword on a tiny clipboard. He had close-cropped gray hair and a good tan, and he was working the puzzle in ink, peering with red-edged eyes through wire-rimmed reading glasses.

We soon struck up a conversation, slightly awkward at first, but gradually less so.

"See those steps?" he asked at one point, gesturing out the window.

"Yes." The train pulled through a kind of outdoor theater with grass and concrete steps.

"There was a photo," he stopped talking, turned to a corrugated cardboard trashcan, and rummaged through it, pulling out the previous day's *Washington Post*. He flipped through the paper and handed me the section folded back.

"A girl from Texas my granddaughter's age with cancer," he said in a low voice, obviously moved by the article.

I glanced at the photo. It was of a young woman and had been taken in the outdoor theater just days before. She had traveled with her family to Virginia for an experimental treatment.

"What kind of cancer?" I asked.

"Are you a doctor?"

"No," I said, "but I know about cancer because my mother has it."

"I'm sorry," he said. "I have Leukemia but it's in total remission."

I looked at him again. He was fairly thin, well put together, with workman's shoes, blue jeans.

"The way you asked, and your appearance," he said, "I thought maybe you were a physician."

"No, I'm a writer and a teacher." I noticed a bullet hole in the glass of the observation car above us. My paranoia did not flare at the sight of it, but it registered for a moment. Something about this man in this setting along with the bullet hole added a slightly ominous dimension to our conversation. There was some open land with a huge house in the distance on a hill, hidden by foliage. He noticed my attention to the landscape.

"Do you know what that is?" he asked.

"No."

"It's Monticello."

I looked again.

"I've taken this trip many times. I'm on my way to my granddaughter's high school graduation in West Virginia. I live in Baltimore. It's easy to drive to DC and take the train from there. Too short a distance to fly. Anyway, the airport is two hours from the town."

I had a sense that I had connected with a raconteur. Easing back into the seat, I wondered if I could keep this civil. A heavyset balding fellow in blue jeans and a crimson sweater with a mustache and bushy eyebrows moved through the car followed by his son. The balding man noticed the pins on my new companion's vest and slowed down enough to ask, "Are you a boy scout leader?"

"These are military decorations," my new friend said, frowning as if offended. "It's Flag Day."

The other man lowered his head and moved by without uttering any apology.

After a moment, I asked, "Where did you serve?"

"In Vietnam."

"What branch?"

"Marines," he said. "That was rude of him."

From the look on his face, I knew he had seen combat and it had taken a lot out of him.

"What do you do now?"

"Semi-retired. But I was an equine photographer."

This explained the many-pocketed vest. Such a specific niche. My curiosity was piqued. "In the sporting sense? You photographed racehorses?"

"Yes, for magazines and newspapers."

"Did you write articles, too?"

"No, not usually. Sometimes I would write captions, but usually, I worked with a writer. There were times where the writer would have photo ideas, or I might have a story angle connected with a series of photos."

"My ex-wife is a racing buff. Did ever you photograph The Derby?"

"Yes. I covered some of the major stories, but mostly I worked for a Baltimore daily doing human interest pieces that sometimes got picked up for syndicated use. I did a piece about a girl that cleaned stables at Churchill Downs. She was the granddaughter of a famous jockey. Those photos ended up everywhere. My editor helped me get pictures of a trainer's family that had ancestors with connections to Irish royalty. I worked with some great editors over the years."

"I heard on NPR about this new book on Seabiscuit."

"Great book," he said, "I just sent the author a drawing of Seabiscuit that hung in my office for years."

"You know her?"

He took a breath, "My editor contacted her publicist. The publicist wouldn't give my editor contact information but passed word on to the author. A famous equine artist who is dead now did the drawing, and it's valuable. The author didn't understand my generosity. I think she thought I was trying to sell it. But it had hung in my office for years, and I just felt like she would get more out of it than I would at this point. I had enjoyed it, but it seemed the thing to do. So she accepted it. I shipped it to her and got a nice thank you note. That was worth it."

I wondered why my new companion in conversation would gift a writer with a drawing out of the blue. I carried this question with me and when I reached Cincinnati and was back at Sitwell's Coffeehouse having breakfast at the counter a few days later, reading *USA Today*, when I saw a photo of the author of the Seabiscuit story under a banner headline. She was a gorgeous blond.

do the retired
military officers
wear their civvies, pins
on their lapels ride trains through
America afraid to
fly knowing air com-
mand intimately fear-
ing risks like elevators
in tall buildings higher than
twelve floors the limit on sur-
vivable freefall?
while the patriots of psychiatric hospitals
re-integrate as train passengers walking between the
cars in fear that they
are still prisoners of some
corporate war al-

ways being relocated,
re-educated, reif-
ied as artists teaching
the retired soldiers to
study war no more.

"My brother-in-law, Ola, was a famous Danish contemporary writer," the photographer continued. "I talked to him often about his writing when I visited my sister. What do you write about?"

"I collect moments," I said. "Lately, the ones that have stirred me have been in performance when I was playing harmonica with a folk group in Cincinnati called Jake Speed and The Freddies. Playing the harmonica involves a set of complex breathing techniques. The breathing calls to mind meditation, and when I think of moments, I feel the breathing that stays calm within them. In writing, I try to capture moments where some situation and combination of ideas meld to generate a story."

He let my words stay in the air, then said, "Ola used to talk about moments. He would get the same tone of voice, the same thrill I hear in you."

"A spiritual advisor of mine tells me that what is real is what perceives the breath, the knower, the presence that is life itself."

He listened intently, nodding his head up and down. I think we both saw what would come next in this conversation, a deeper degree of intimacy. I wondered if we talked about Vietnam and war would I boil with anger. He had no idea that I had been in Trenton State Mental Hospital for three weeks. The Geodon appeared to be holding me now. All that had changed with the new medication was the schedule. I was taking it in the morning instead of at bedtime. The train moved, swaying from side to side, through the sunny, wooded Virginia hills.

"My favorite Vietnam novel," I said, "is *Going After Cacciato* by Tim O'Brien. *The Things They Carried* is powerful, too."

Before he could respond I let my thoughts lead me into a meditation: Is it ignorance that causes conflicts? Are they premeditated? Why should tolerance be so necessary with each breath? Why was I caught in this field of attachment? There have always been wars. There will always be wars. Maybe I just needed to stop caring and take the perspective of George Carlin, who said something like, "If people want to kill each other, let 'em. I can't control other people. My role is just to point out what's funny about it."

I think I said something like that to this new acquaintance on the train as I was finding another side of myself.

"Do you have any interest in teaching a course on Vietnam literature?" he asked.

"No. Not that I'm not interested, but my focus has been on homeless literature. The connection to Vietnam tends to be when the homeless veteran enters my field. Miss America has taken the homeless veteran problem as her issue, but I don't know of any literature that connects the Vietnam veteran and homelessness. Most of the veterans I've come across have been socially and economically integrated into society."

"When you teach homeless literature what texts do you use?"

"There are many, ranging from personal accounts like Lars Eighner's to George Orwell's memoir from the thirties. I include a counter-culture classic by Gurney Norman from the seventies and the Buddhist perspective by essayist Gary Snyder. I'm still developing the course idea and I hope to teach after I finish my degree. Currently, I don't have a teaching job; I'm finishing my thesis memoir." I think I was beginning to bore him. Or maybe I was the one losing interest.

"I'm gonna go take a smoke," my companion said, excusing himself and heading for the smoking car. I had passed by it before. It was half of a car with ashtrays and haze. It reminded me of the smoking rooms in mental institutions.

In his absence, I found myself thinking of one of my favorite films from my adolescence, *King of Hearts*. In it, a French town is occupied by Germans in World War I while the insane asylum inmates are accidentally let loose to populate the village after the rest of the townsfolk flee. It's a touching and humorous film, and the conclusion seems to indicate that the insane are gentler and healthier than the sane. I had sometimes wondered about this, but my counselor had assured me that in fact when I was off my medication, I was at risk of doing myself or others harm. I hadn't brought all this into the conversation with the photographer. I was aware that I was still out of balance though I was managing however precariously to stay away from trouble for now. But with my new companion gone, I grew uneasy and decided to go to the dining car for dinner.

I sat down at a table with a middle-aged woman with short, mousy brown hair. She introduced herself as a retired, prison guard from Oregon who had left her job to travel around America by Amtrak and was now facing the prospect of returning home and finding another job. I don't remember much about her traveling companion except that she was heavier and that they seemed to be a couple.

There was also a man across from me, who was balding, thin, and wearing a pale blue cardigan sweater. He took off his horn-rimmed glasses and while wiping them on a white handkerchief told us about the rolling White House on this track and the WW II hidden bunkers on this train's run.

As I listened, I wondered if the current government had an official train and if the retired officers who traveled by Amtrak were in service still, or if they rode the train because they were frightened of air travel. It came as a flash of conspiracy theory; discomforting and setting my paranoid thoughts afire for a few minutes.

I ate my steak and potato without saying much about myself. I sensed that if I did disclose who I was, I'd be just like them; and that might have been better than feeling what I felt, that I wasn't capable of being a healthy member of this society with its necessary right-wing hypocrisy. My anxiety now kept me from riding elevators in buildings taller than twelve stories. I would always ask when entering a modern skyscraper, is there a way to do this by stairs?

After dining with these three (and never learning what the bald man did for a living), I paced back through the rocking train cars to my seat where I returned to reading Margaret Atwood and dozing. The photographer had apparently disembarked at one of the small towns in West Virginia while I was gone.

As it got dark, it got harder to read. The lights kept failing when the train stopped for fuel and water and other reasons that were never explained. I talked briefly with a couple across the aisle. The man was a bit of a long hair and turned out to be a composer returning to make his dissertation defense at the College Conservatory of Music in Cincinnati. His wife had an Eastern European accent. We talked until we tired of things to say, with a mutual sigh, we all sat still as the train bumped slowly along that final turn over the dark Ohio River.

It had been nearly twenty years since I had stayed in a facility as rough as Trenton. I had told myself then that if faced with a state facility again, I'd rather take my own life. Here I was, not thinking such thoughts at all, was just relieved that Dr. Nuñez had risked keeping me on Geodon. It was mostly a matter of adjustment. I would see my counselor in Cincinnati. I would finish the reading list, take my oral exam for my Master's degree and then get a teaching job.

A sense of relief swept through me when the train stopped at Union Terminal. In the dark Cincinnati morning, my gray Toyota shone in the amber streetlight of the empty parking lot. I threw my brown pack into the cluttered trunk, then unlocked the driver's side door. As I sat down, I saw the dead daisy. It had withered and stuck to the side of the clear Stewart's Orange Creamsicle bottle in the drink holder between seats.

12

Lacey #5

LOOKING LIKE A PIXIE, with her thin curvy body, piercings, long-lashed blue eyes, long brown hair tucked into two pigtail braids tied with red ribbons, she lay on her belly, elbows propped on the sidewalk, one of my discarded harmonicas at her lips. She swung her bare feet above her waist, Capri cut jeans showing plenty of clean-shaven ankle. Seven in the evening with the summer sun slanting over the roof of the ice cream shop on the corner across the street, her position seemed odd to me, mostly because it was such a public place and she seemed so at home.

I wanted very badly to know what she was up to, but did not want to interrupt her idyll as her mouth moved against the chrome and black plastic while the reeds vibrated in a simple pattern; she was playing *Skip to My Lou*, but one note clunked each time, the blown reed, the reason I had discarded the instrument. Impressed by her ability to find the tune without one of the notes, and play it with such innocence, I sat down, my back to the painted, red brick building, crossed my legs, and felt the gritty concrete sidewalk with the palms of my big hands.

"Do you think my performance was better than a D?" Lacey asked.

"Yes. But it doesn't matter what I think," I said, "I'm sorry."

"Yeah." She pinched her nose with her hand and grimaced.

"Did you go talk to the teacher?"

"I made an appointment for tomorrow."

"How did you do in the rest of the class?"

"I missed an assignment. She said on the eval that I hadn't taken each of the elements of acting the scene into consideration. And she didn't like the soliloquy I selected."

"Were you required to get the selection approved ahead of time?"

"Yes."

"Did she approve it?"

"That was the assignment I missed."

"Lace. You have to talk to her."

"She's my advisor, and she's being hard on me for no reason." I could feel the tremor in her voice.

"If I knew I was getting a D in the course, I would have dropped it and saved the money. She knows I'm paying for it myself."

She stood, took my hand, lifted me to my feet. We held hands for a long minute, and she said, "God it sucks that you were in for a month."

I wanted to tell her about the basketball, the strange Disney fantasy dreams, the Memorial Day grill out. We had big pieces of chicken without any seasoning. I wanted to cry with relief.

"Was it terrible?"

"You can't imagine," I said.

We were sitting at a table in front of Sitwell's now. I saw the fine dark hair on her forearm. "I like your harmonica," I said.

She hummed a little bit of *Skip*. "I wanted to come get you out. They wouldn't give me a straight answer on the phone."

"Yeah," I said. "I know."

"Was it really bad?" she asked.

"This guy, Stu, one of the social workers, said they had my height as six foot seven inches."

She smiled, laughed a little. "That's fucked."

"Yeah."

She got up, took my hand, and pirouetted on the sidewalk.

I felt so tied up inside. I didn't have the words to say how scared and happy I was, how much I wanted to spend more time with her.

Lacey's girlfriend, Kerrie came out of the coffeehouse. Kerrie had a pierced nose and many earrings. Her nail polish was black, her lipstick dark blue. Kerrie's curly light brown hair was tossed up into a wrap on her head. She always wore the same black tank top and torn indigo jeans with blue ballpoint inkings scrawled on the tops of the thighs. Kerrie had a bent back and thin, pale arms.

"Lacey, we have to go," she said, lighting a cigarette and handing it to Lacey, getting between us.

"Just a minute." Lacey turned back to me. "What do I do?"

"Go to the appointment tomorrow and ask if you can do some extra work, something that she approves beforehand."

Sometimes I thought Lacey was satirizing me. How could she not see her patterns? Or else she was melting away into my madness.

13

My Feet Are Two Different Sizes

MER WAS A FRIEND of mine who taught English at a secular private high school. Nearly thirty, with short-cropped dark hair, intense warm brown eyes, a short straight nose, Mer had empathy for the struggles of her students, having experienced her share of teenage angst and being still a little self-conscious about her weight as an adult. I first met Mer at Sitwell's Coffeehouse as I was coming out of my marriage, and we became fast friends.

As I started graduate school, she was one of my key supports. I'd help her grade papers and she'd help me with research on papers I was writing. We'd pulled a couple of all-nighters together working on her grading, and we also shared strong support for some of Sitwell's regulars whom we'd helped prepare for the SATs. Mer moonlighted for a company that gave SAT training to high schoolers.

It had been a while since we'd seen each other, but I called to see if she would go shopping with me. After the trip to New York City, the shoe problem was still very much on my mind, and as should be clear by now, I desperately needed help in that department.

As I planned another trip, this time to Vermont to visit my brother and his family, I still didn't have a good pair of walking shoes. For years I'd used leather-soled wingtips for walking, but now I was thinking I'd try a newer design. The left shoe of my best pair of wingtips seemed to be getting tighter. I got on the Internet at the new Sitwell's late one night when the regulars were the only customers. John Stamstead, one of Cincinnati's finest cyclists, an ultra-marathoner, had done a magazine ad for Rockports. I decided to try their walking shoes. If a great cyclist liked them, maybe they were okay. So, I checked out the different designs and found a store in Northern Kentucky that carried the ones I liked in brown leather with round toes and air-cushioned rubber soles.

The plan was to pick up Mer downtown at her beau's place. He drove a Jaguar and did some kind of public relations writing for some conservative causes. I was starting to wonder about Mer's politics, but that wasn't the thing.

The thing was I snagged some flowers out of a round, concrete, streetside planter for my car. I now had an orange lily and a white daisy in a bottle in the drink holder. Mer was her smiling self at her boyfriend's. I went in, got a hug from her, and a tour of the first-floor business area, with its high ceilings, gray walls, dark-stained woodwork, tile floors, and marble mantles. Suddenly we were driving, and I was intoxicated with Mer's presence. I drove through Fort Washington Way where the new stadiums were under construction. I got lost, but with the sunroof and Mer chatting away, I felt warm, loved, and as if I were buzzing on some exotic drug. The breeze blew through me, around me, and in me. My thoughts were dusty with Mer's plumeria scent.

"What are we shopping for?"

"Well, Mer, it's funny. We're shopping for shoes. I have a bit of a problem. My feet are two different sizes. I read somewhere that Greg LeMond, the champion cyclist, has the same problem. One foot is a full size larger than the other is. He has custom shoes from an endorsement. I should buy two different pairs of shoes, just to have one pair."

"Do you really buy two pairs?"

"Is it pairs or pair?"

"Two English teachers with one good question."

"Yeah. I just buy for the left foot. It's bigger."

"OK."

"Then I want to go to this new bike shop I saw advertised in *CityBeat*. They have Colnago hats."

"What are Colnago hats?"

"You'll see."

When we found the shoe outlet in Newport, it had a small driveway with space for five cars in front. The interior had low light and a cramped feeling. Coming into the air conditioning, I felt a slight chill. As we walked in, there they were. The exact shoes I wanted in my left foot's size, right there on the carpeted floor by a low mirror just left of the entry. It was as if the Internet research I had done had been transmitted to the store. I tried them on, and they were comfortable, springy, and transcendent for the foot. Ahh, but I needed this. My right foot was a full size smaller than my left, and honestly, the right shoe felt a bit big. I asked the clerk for a smaller size. She led us to the floor-to-ceiling shelves in back where I looked at other designs. Nothing looked right. She brought out a smaller pair of the same shoe and I tried them on. By now we were behind a curtain in the back right area of the shop. Here I could sit on a leather stuffed bench to tie the laces. The smaller shoe fit my right foot perfectly. The left was too tight. The narrow, shoe-stacked room smelled of leather and cleaning solution. It seemed to close in on me. I felt perspiration on my arms and chest.

Mer said, "No one would know," and giggled.

I smiled. "You think so?" She shook her head gazing at me, then past me, then at the floor.

I put the larger of the left shoes back on my left foot then put the smaller one in the box with the larger right shoe. We walked up to the counter by the door.

"I'll wear them," I said.

There was a thin-faced lady clerk, with lipstick that edged larger than her lips. She moved deliberately but had a herky-jerky motion when she pulled the socks off the display behind her.

"One of those. Two of those. One of those," I went on until I selected forty-five dollars' worth of thin dark dress socks.

"Cash or charge?" she asked.

"I'll charge it."

She filled out a receipt with a pen after running the card through an old-fashioned imprinter. Mer wiggled from foot to foot, grinning a bit while we waited.

"Bike shop next," I said.

We walked out into the sweltering humidity. The afternoon had heated up. I unlocked the gray Toyota, keyed the ignition,

and flipped on the A/C. Mer laughed then stopped and put her
hand on my leg. When I turned toward her, she shook her head.
A tap came on the window. It was the lady clerk. I lowered the
electric window, feeling my ears get hot.

"It looks like you took two different size shoes," she said.

"Ohh," I said. "I'd actually like to buy both pairs. Here's my
credit card." I handed her the card through the window.

"Well, I got caught," I said to Mer. "It turned out okay. She was
nice about it."

Mer was quiet, then said, "It shocked me when she came out."
"Yeah."

The air conditioner droned. The car interior cooled. We were
no longer giddy and laughing. Mer and I had opened a door
together. Our friendship would be altered. I thought about what
I had done and felt guilt and remorse.

"I shouldn't have done that. It was wrong."

"It seemed rather harmless."

"They ought to sell shoes singly. You would think some
Internet company would come up with a way to get a pair of
shoes that are different sizes. There have to be a lot of people
with the same need."

"We almost got away with it."

"Well. I can afford both pairs. I'll wear thinner socks with the
smaller pair. Or none."

"Are you sure you can afford both?"

I sat silent for a minute. I could have gone inside, taken off
the smaller shoe and made the larger pair a pair again. I was
embarrassed.

"Yep."

The lady came out with the shoes, a blue pen, and the receipt
to sign. I signed and was careful to return her pen before closing
the window again.

She didn't say anything when she handed over the box. I
felt bad. Even in the cool car, I was sweating. My black cotton
button-down shirt clung to me. The gray and maroon cloth car
seat was wet. I didn't like myself a whole lot. Mer sat deflated.
Her face had lost its joy.

I drove over to Monmouth Street looking for the bike shop.
Mer spotted it first. I went past and had to turn around. We
were walking down the street together while my steps sprung up
and down from the new shoes. They made cricket-like sounds

because of the air-filled insoles. In the cluttered, well-lit shop I found a pink, yellow and blue Colnago racing cap. It had club symbols on it. When I showed it to Mer, she laughed. The hat fit. There were racks and racks of jerseys. Then I bought two yellow jerseys, one long sleeve, and one short sleeve. I wondered what Mer thought about my spending. She didn't say a word. In the rear of the store hi-tech top-of-the-line racing bikes nestled on chrome stands side-by-side. The new technology looked so ultra-lite and fragile to a large cyclist like me. I chatted with the owner who seemed to recognize my name from my credit card. I like to think I'm a known cyclist in the area, and he asked me where I had been, as if I'd been away. I told him I hadn't been riding that actively but was getting back to it in Clifton.

Back in the Toyota, Mer and I sped over the Licking River back to Covington, crossed the Ohio on the Suspension Bridge with the steel deck singing under the tires.

"Do you like the lily?" I asked.

"Pretty color," she said.

"I lifted it from a streetside planter in O'Bryanville," I laughed.

She smiled but her eyebrows flattened. There was an awkward quiet and I thought about turning on the radio or flipping in a Bob Dylan tape. Instead, I looked ahead and tried to watch Mer in my peripheral vision. She leaned away from me into the seat. Her eyes cast down, I could see the faint eye-shadow and a fold of skin at her jaw.

I found my way through the roadways that were still under construction swinging around corners, rocking the car, still fascinated with Mer's essence, her plumeria scent spinning in my head. We arrived back at her door on Ninth Street exactly an hour and ten minutes from when I picked her up.

Saying goodbye, I reached around her to squeeze, and kissed her warmly on the cheek, trying to find her lips. She squirmed away, obviously uncomfortable. I haven't seen her since.

14

BURLINGTON AND
BEYOND

June 20, 2001

Alan,
Hi! I'm writing from Cinci where I am planning a
visit to Vermont in two weeks. I am considering
taking VIA rail from Montreal to Chicago with a
stopover in Toronto between the 8th and 10th of
July. Let me hear from you if you will be around and
are interested in a visit. I'm finishing grad school
this summer writing a thesis novel and reading
many books. In the fall, I hope to be teaching
or starting another graduate degree. My brother
Rigo and his family are in Burlington, VT. I have
booked air travel both ways but find trains more
comfortable and the opportunity to see Toronto
again, after so many years, is enticing. Let me hear
from you.
peace,
Steve

June 21, 2001

Steven,
We will be around between the 8th and the 10th.
We are always interested in visits, or we have a
guest room if you would like to stay with us. You
might hear a crying baby from time to time (Paul
is now 7 months old) but aside from that, it is
comfortable and a good base for touring Toronto
(about a 10-minute walk from the subway). Please
let me know your plans.
Alan

June 22, 2001

Alan,
Any good Chinese restaurants around the train
station? I'm interested in visiting and would love
to meet your young prodigy. A crying baby would
be a welcome sound after all the chatting I've been
doing trying to deal with local beer heads and
smokers. I'm trying to find Margaret Atwood. I'm
reading her book and am interested in stealing her
ideas. Simple people write books, stupid people
steal, easy goes it. I'm kidding about taking ideas,
but I listen to friends and I'd like to know what
Paul's schedule is like, so I can compare to a friend
who might be delivered on or about the date I'll
be visiting. Coming through Montreal. Planning
to cross Lake Champlain on a ferry, weather
permitting, board at Port Kent or Plattsburg. Can I
bring you any consumable items from Cincinnati?
Can you get bagels? Lox? Bruegger's is around the
corner, and they're good. I've heard there are cycle
shops in Toronto. Any sew-up tires at good prices
might be worth returning with. What's the weather
like? I think it's 11 to 14 here but I've never been
able to do the centigrade conversion in my head.

Is your apartment near the lake?
Thanks for your help.
Innocently,
Steve

June 23, 2001

Steve,
There are many good Chinese restaurants in
Toronto, but I am not sure which are the good
ones now. I will have to check. Most of them
are downtown, not that far from the train station,
but too far if you are carrying any bags. We live
in a house somewhat uptown, but convenient
to downtown. You can get anywhere by subway,
which goes to the train station and also is about
a 10- to 15-minute walk from the house. I am not
sure where Margaret is hanging these days. Paul's
schedule is not like anything they warn you about
before you have kids. Usually, it is not that bad, but
this week is not a good one to ask about. He has
been getting over a cold and is teething, and wakes
up about every 3 hours during the night. Hopefully,
by next week he will be back to normal....sleep
9 to about 8 (waking up once or twice at the
most) and then 2 naps during the day. I crossed
Lake Champlain once at Plattsburg, in the winter.
It wasn't too nice, but I think it will be for you.
No consumable items from Cinci are necessary.
Toronto has all of that stuff...it is one of the more
ethnically diversified cities around. July weather
could be hot and humid, but not quite as humid as
Cinci. Days will be between the 70s and 90s. Nights
should be low 60s. Let me know exactly when you
plan to arrive so I can make arrangements (we go
away on weekends).
Alan

June 24, 2001

Alan,
I'm going to be arriving in Toronto early in the
morning on Monday the ninth of July. I plan to
leave the next day at six a.m., arrive in Chicago
on the eleventh, have a full day in Chicago, and
then return to Cincinnati early morning of Friday,
July twelfth/thirteenth. I plan to be carrying a rare
instrument in a large case, a small backpack, and a
briefcase. The train is a sleeper and travels slowly
and quietly overnight. It's scheduled for departure
after eleven and arrival around eight-thirty in the
morning. If it would help I can have breakfast
around nine and meet you later in the morning.
I'd love to see the lake, but I'm more interested
in Margaret Atwood. These are two addresses and
phone #s for M. Atwood's in Toronto.
M Atwood 3800 Yonge St Toronto, ON M4N 3P7
Phone: xxx-xxx-xxxx M D Atwood 1 Garden Ave
Toronto, ON M6R 1H5 Phone: xxx-xxx-xxxx
If you do get a chance to talk to her before I
do, please tell her I'm interested in any research
she might know of on the size of root vegetables
and apples from the setting of *Alias Grace* in the
Belleville area. I'm going to try to find farmer's
almanacs, but the whole story isn't told in statistics.
Her account so fascinated me that I've decided to
write an article about it. My brother in Vermont
grows leafy greens in a garden and is involved with
tomato nurseries. I'm curious about comparison
studies and regional differences. But, because I
cycled through that region in 1975 and again in
1976, I think I'm qualified to do the research that
involves meeting in public and touching on the
tricky issues that this kind of inquiry might open. If
you read *Alias Grace*, you'll immediately recognize
that the psychological implications of the medical
research implied so much transference that a
more careful analysis of hand size, physiological

development, and masturbation might be the sources of the objectification of the woman who ended up in New England and died around the time of the Great War. The question of hypnotism and mesmerism seems to be no more than a quarrel between id and superego while the ego stands in check.

I'd explain all this in a letter on letterhead, but there isn't time. If she needs a reference from Miami University, ask her to talk to Jerry Rosenberg, who by all accounts is an Atwood scholar.

I apologize for asking you to go between for me. My phone number in Cincinnati is xxx-xxx-xxxx. If you want to talk to me about this, email me, and we'll schedule a conversation.

It would help to have your address and a web address for the subway system in Toronto before I leave on the third. Maybe you could give me an idea which line you are on and how to change, etc. I'd rather travel above ground if there are buses, but since I'll be traveling alone, and you know the customs better than I do, I'll follow your advice. They tell me the train station is on Front Street. I'm looking forward with pleasure to seeing your home and family together.

My departure is delayable by a day if weather or other problems come up.

all best,

Steve

***

As I REEXAMINE THIS exchange of emails now, I feel ashamed. I cannot imagine what Alan thought of me. It's a sad thing to accept how ill I was, and how strangely obsessed I was with a sense of my own ego.

My dad had offered me an Eames chair before I left for New York and my unplanned month in New Jersey. I needed help moving the chair to my apartment from their place, but he had stopped speaking to me, even after I paid him back the rent he had covered during my absence.

My friend Karen, who was Lacey's age, and was studying French at the University of Cincinnati, heard me mention the chair one day while I was sitting on the bench outside Sitwell's. Karen worked part time at the ice cream shop on the corner near Sitwell's and was hanging outside with me on a cigarette break. She offered to let me use her truck and came along for the ride so she could hold the elevator door. She assured Dad she was a professional as she carried the foot of the chair. That's how Dad referred to her after that, as "the professional."

Karen had no way of knowing what I had been through, and I didn't let on. I didn't particularly feel guilty for my behavior and thinking. I had spots. Real ones. The Haldol illuminated and helped lift me from the poverty of madness. But the Geodon kept me on an edge that felt good. Keeping my dad unsettled hurt me emotionally. At the same time, I derived satisfaction from it. In the past, when he'd felt he had the upper hand with me, he'd dictated to my women friends in my presence a standard line that went something like this: "Good to get to meet you. You are welcome here, even if you are not welcome in Steve's life at some point." This was often delivered over a shared meal after Dad had had a few or was feeling a measure of smugness. It would fill me with shame.

Now, I realize how much I resented him for such behavior. But I also have a clearer window into why he acted the way he did. With the edge from the Geodon checking me for the moment from acting on my resentment, Karen kept him at a distance. Aware of the tension between Dad and me, she was cool towards him, warm to me, but also giving him his due. Hers was a stiff dance. Mom had given up her garden in Clifton when they sold the house, but Karen commented to Dad on Mom's pink geraniums, potted in black ceramic planters inside the apartment door, saying, "I love those."

PART 2

Steven
May 1, 2020

15

Rigo, My Brother, My Brother

A MAN WITH A buzzing silver electric wand touched me through my clothes. I told myself to stay calm and breathe. This was July 2001, and I was flying United. It would be two months before terrorists hijacked jets and crashed them into the Twin Towers, but I was scared because I had caught a glimpse of the pilots as I boarded, and they seemed very young. On the one-hour flight to Chicago, which arrived at the exact same time it left because of time-zone differences, I ate dried fruit from a sticky plastic bag. I was caught up in time travel thoughts. Every moment registered as time passing and not passing. I felt a celestial shift.

Deplaning, I saw the pilots again. One had a beard, the other a bushy mustache. They had been clean shaven; now they had crow's feet at the corners of their eyes. They had aged ten years in an hour. I was sure something freaky had happened to the spheres.

In the airport bar, I ate cheesy, thick-crust, Chicago-style pizza, and gulped cola. When I got on the connecting flight to Burlington, I was even more scared. My mind kept playing Rigo's rejection over and over. I tried to remember his exact words on the phone. He had quizzed me about the dosage of my medication, asking me to explain decompensation symptoms. I stayed calm then. He had not asked about the past few weeks, and I had not told him. But I was sure Dad had mentioned the hospitalization in Trenton, even though I felt it was none of Rigo's business.

Rigo probed my medical situation like he was a clinician, or a doctor, and then said, "I don't want you to come."

I blew up on the phone and cursed him. The rejection stung.

I knew my brother was wealthy and materialistic, a scientist and outdoor enthusiast. I was sure the reason he didn't want me in Vermont was that he was afraid of what I would see.

I had called several music stores long distance to ask whether they would evaluate a lute for insurance purposes. The owner of the Burlington Violin Shop responded angrily, "I don't want to see that kind of instrument." I decided he was a snob. He didn't say why he wouldn't look at my lute, but I guessed he preferred to handle classical orchestral instruments. I talked to a young woman at another store and found myself imagining meeting her. I asked Rigo for help with this, but he never responded. I feared that he'd think I was buying it for his daughter. I wasn't. I just wanted her to see her uncle with it, to hear his hands play across the strings. I couldn't explain this to Rigo. He wouldn't understand.

I arrived in Burlington on a Wednesday, my night back home to play harmonica with Jake Speed and the Freddies at Cody's coffeehouse.

I took a taxi from the airport into town because the buses didn't run on holidays. At a coffeehouse on the north edge of the business district, I read the weekly and daily papers and my suspicions and paranoia about Rigo filled me like a flame. Rigo was working an experiment. He ran advertisements in at least three daily papers, offered huge sums for experimental subjects, told them they could be paid to smoke marijuana, then tracked their buying habits with computer-assisted software from companies in Vermont, and once they were so fully psychologically addicted, withdrew their marijuana supply. The homeless problem was Rigo's experiment. Addicts were blamed and suffered. I had been through substance abuse treatment, and now I was dependent on psychotropics instead of marijuana.

Either way, I was controlled. I was a monitored being. Rigo knew my conundrum and was protecting himself and his way of life like he had in San Francisco in 1978. Reject Steve, say no. He didn't want to have to deal with me directly on the medication issue.

16

RIGO AND HIS WIFE, AFRAID

BANKING STORIES WILL PROBABLY never make headlines. I could open an account without a fee in another state if I used a minor as the principal owner of the money. I called Rigo from the bank in downtown Burlington, check in hand, and asked his daughter's Social Security number. He hung up on me.

I pumped myself up and decided to open a smaller account for myself, leave Laurie's name on the account with mine, and deal with her father later. I could add to the account with a transfer from a distance in a week when I could sit in my own living room and think things over a little more clearly. The banker said it would cost five dollars a month to keep the account open if the balance fell under five hundred dollars. I left dejected. I didn't have the decency to leave a thousand dollars.

Later that day I talked to Rigo's wife on the bus. Through synchronicity, I'd bumped into her. She had her bicycle on the bus's bike rack. We exited together. While she walked her bike up the hill, and I paced her, I explained, "My ex and I had a small sum in a shared account leftover from our time together, and to atone for the "sins of the father" I'd like to open an account in Laurie's name and be custodian."

"It's tainted money," she said.

I said, "Okay," and turned and walked away.

It was hard. I was uncovering real-life situations that outdid Atwood's novel. Yet I had no confidant, no one to ratify my feelings. The trip to Vermont had been a forced thing. I'd felt reluctantly pulled, as I had been to New York. Risk attracted me, though the girls in Cincinnati were a counter-magnetic force. But I'd heard a call. I believed it came from above. Rigo discouraged this kind of thinking. He'd offered to buy out my ticket so that I wouldn't have to come. When he said that, after we'd talked in a better moment about sailing together on his boat, I said, "I never want to set foot on that fucking boat again."

He also failed to understand the lute. We used to joke years ago about "getting the loot," and I had transmogrified it into a lute, teasing Rigo that he could build one. He didn't get the joke now or had forgotten. But I ordered one from Indonesia anyway and had it shipped to his house. "You didn't buy that for Laurie, did you?" he asked.

When I arrived, he was holding the UPS box, which he handed over without a word. I wanted to cry but I didn't want to let him see, so I took the box and left, carrying it on my shoulder, shifting it from side to side, back to the Lang House, a nice bed-and-breakfast, where I got a room for the night.

> July 6, 2001
> Steve,
> Sorry it took so long to respond. We have been away out in western Canada and just got back yesterday. I was just reading in the paper this morning about Mordecai Richler's death and saw that Margaret Atwood was very shaken up about it, so I do not think this is going to be a good time to contact her. It also turns out that we are not going to be here next week. We were planning to go away for the weekend but now plan on stretching that into next week. Sorry about that. One hotel downtown that I believe is reasonable (many in Toronto are not) is the Executive Motor Hotel at 621 King Street West (416-504-7441). Also, I know there are lots of B&B's, only I don't know where they are but you may try www.toronto.com for listings. That site might also have a subway map.
> Sorry we will miss you, but perhaps we will see you

at St. Joe's later this summer (we are heading up
later in July for 2 weeks).
Regards,
Alan

17

CUSTOMS

THE MORNING I LEFT Burlington, I went to the bank. They refused my bank check from Columbia Savings in Cincinnati, so I decided to get a cash advance and some Canadian currency instead. I walked back via the library, checked out nothing, but looked at a biography of Mordecai Richler written during the Trudeau years.

Back at the B & B, I packed up, took the music case in one hand, then hiked into town, with the brown rucksack on my shoulders. I was dressed well, putting on the dog for my walk, wearing my gray alpaca wool vest and the fine Peterman Nat Wednesday coat. I bought a ticket for the ferry as the clouds pranced like sheep across the pale blue. While I waited to board, I had an iced decaf, the first coffee drink I'd had since leaving Sitwell's in Cincinnati.

As we got underway, I ate my remaining dates, spitting the pits into the water over the white painted railing. I figured if I were going to Canada, I didn't want to have anything at the border that might be a problem. After a pleasant crossing, I walked from the landing up the hill to the Port Kent bus depot and train tracks. While I was talking to the ticket agent making a reservation from Plattsburgh to Montreal for tomorrow, the bus appeared, as if it had been cloaked in from another dimension. I spoke in person with the two Amtrak officials in charge, a driver and a porter with an Aceola badge. The porter, who had a flip haircut and a rather pear-shaped black girl's butt, explained that because Amtrak had some sort of problem, a bus had replaced the train on this route today. They accepted me as a walk-on. The bus driver wanted me to put the instrument case in the luggage locker, but he let me take it on the very empty bus. There was an older couple, and two young men speaking French. I was the odd man out. My jeans were torn, my long gray hair down, and I looked rather conspicuous.

I remembered another visit to Plattsburgh. There were always bridges down and up, making navigation tricky. From the window, it looked as if the city might be a war zone. We passed some very impressive complexes and what might have been a fort or a detention center. A lot of red brick buildings.

When we reached the border, the driver turned, his big red face under a blue hat, and said, "Everybody off the bus for customs. Bring all your luggage."

I walked through the aisle, olive green square-rigger bag in one hand and deep blue lute case in the other. My brown rucksack hugged my shoulders. There was a queue in the low-ceilinged building with a line on the floor marking where I was to stand when it came my turn. Fluorescent lamps blazed. The woman immigration official looked Asian, with black hair and dark eyes. I gave her my passport, and she asked me where I was going.

"Montreal. Then I plan to take the train to Toronto and back to Chicago."

"What is the purpose of your visit to Canada?"

I thought of my Siberian girlfriend, Anastasia Romanova, as the woman smiled.

"I'm on vacation, but I'm a freelance writer and plan to write on my trip. I'm hoping to meet the writer, Margaret Atwood, in Toronto."

"How long do you expect to be in Canada?"

"No more than a couple of weeks, probably nine days or so."

"Do you have friends in Canada?"

"No." This was a lie. I knew a number of Canadians and Americans who visited Canada in the summer.

"What do you do for a living?"

"I'm a freelance writer."

"Do you have a return ticket?"

"No, I don't."

"How much money do you have with you?"

"I have around three hundred dollars American and two hundred Canadian. I also have several credit cards."

She jumped in at that point with a question I wasn't expecting. "Have you ever been convicted of a crime?" Now, she wasn't smiling, she was tapping my marrow with imploring brown eyes.

I paused for a moment. "I've been arrested but the charges were dropped. Once, I was stopped in Arizona for stealing gasoline and I spent the night in jail."

"What else were you arrested for?"

"I took a car."

"Have you been to court?"

"I've been for psychiatric reasons in the past."

"Do you know you have a SID number?"

"No. What is that?"

"It indicates you have a criminal record. You are not welcome in Canada. Wait here and someone will take you back to the U.S. Customs Center."

The walls closed in, making the room stuffy and warm. I began to sweat.

"I'm a schizophrenic, and I take medication, but I'm not crazy."

"You are not a genuine visitor. You are being refused entry to Canada."

"Is there anything I can do to resolve this?"

"I will give you a form to file with Immigration. You will need to list any arrests, court appearances and convictions."

I was scared. Sure that some of this was because Dad had some tax scheme going with his land on St. Joseph Island, Ontario. I didn't want to tell this woman that I had a summer cottage, because I was afraid that Dad would get in trouble, or that I would get in worse trouble with Dad.

Journal Entry, July 7, 2001

I was turned back from the border. There was this young immigration official, a Siberian Princess. I waited for a bus to Plattsburgh, with no idea what to do next, but I planned and waited, while writing and looking at the brownish red-tile floor. I showed one of the Treasury Officials some old two-dollar bills with Monticello on the back. She claimed it was the first time she had seen such a thing. The young lady at the Canadian border gave me a stupid form to fill out. I took it back to the U.S. side and filled it out, returned it to her, and she still said no entry.

I asked a U.S. Immigration Official if I could get Diplomatic Immunity or some kind of State Department Temporary Appointment. He said he couldn't help. He was very respectful. The U.S. Officials were all kind, and seemed competent. But they they couldn't affect anything on the Canadian side.

I was thinking it might be for my own protection. Which scared me more than anything. It was a shitty day when you couldn't get a shower or something decent to eat before one a.m.

At two-thirty on Sunday morning, I decided to walk into a war memorial. Instinct took me to the lakeside. I had a déjà vu. There were brick steps and a dewy lawn. I found a large pyramidal stone marker with rough edges and laid my gear around me, putting on all my shirts, jackets, vest, and the Nat Wednesday jacket again. I slept outdoors for the first time in years.

The moon was just beginning to wane as the night passed, growing mistier. The lake was calm. A gaggle of gray geese, not Canada Geese, woke me, climbing, squalling, and parading past me onto the memorial in the early morning light. A couple of men were waiting for the geese. I got up, gathered my gear, a bit embarrassed, and walked up to the memorial. There were no signs anywhere saying that the park was closed or listing any hours. Thank God for American War Heroes and memorials that never close.

I hiked into the town and found one big neon blue "Open" sign on a sweeping corner. It was a taxi dispatch. I asked if there was a public restroom. I went in and took a shit the Krishna way. No TP. Grungy. The rest of the morning was a struggle. Sleepy, dehydrated, scared, and fighting to stay calm and cool, I asked at the taxi dispatch for a B&B when I returned there a few hours later after watching the town wake up. The B&B, dispatch told me, was at twenty-nine and he named the street, I don't remember the name he gave, but as I walked this weird little woman, with a cap, and close-cropped hair appeared and started to walk with me, asking if she could help. I told her the street name, the number twenty-nine, and followed her. She had a Walkman pinned to her ears, and her eyes were beady and brown. She spoke in a voice that sounded damaged, like her voice box had been stepped on. Was her voice mechanical because she was hearing what to say in her earpiece? She paced me across a bridge. The neighborhood got cleaner and the houses larger and more manicured.

Even though I smelled a con, when she shouted to me that she had found the B&B, I let her lead me to a door across the street. It was almost seven in the morning. I heard a little voice in my head say, tip her two, so I gave her a two-dollar bill and she told me to have a good day in a way that struck me as suspiciously gratuitous. Then, as I stood at the door waiting, looking up at the green shutters, a very wicked-looking woman appeared. She had a thin witch face. She could have been Elphaba. Her teeth looked dirty and mean. With a haughty look, she claimed not to have a room and offered to call a taxi.

I thanked her and waited a minute before walking to the train station where the bus had turned around on the way from Port Kent to the border. I had the train reservation I had made yesterday. This whole area was beginning to smell like bad fish. The sky was perfectly blue, the clouds were walking with me, and the breeze had an intoxicating sense of impending doom.

I think this occurred to me much later, but it is important to place it here. Perhaps some power was guiding me to the key locations for my study of *Alias Grace*. Maybe the B&B in Plattsburgh was the place where the title character, Grace Marks, a celebrated murderess, had relocated from Canada after serving her time.

What if when mentioning Margaret Atwood at the border I had been overheard, and now people were conspiring to help me show the truth about the history of Grace? I think, in my deluded state, I believed that my thoughts were being broadcast so that others knew all or part of what I was thinking. How much of what I was discovering was guided? Did I have free will? The film needed a train ride through the wilderness where I had ridden the bus the day before. Remember back in Sitwell's? Alex had insisted he wanted me to write a scene on a train. Could Alex be the director? The psychiatrist in Atwood's novel traveled to and from Kingston, Ontario by passenger train. Perhaps those scenes were to be shot next? Had I been cast in the role of psychiatrist? Were the scenes in Trenton going to be used to show me as a psychiatrist working a psychiatry rotation?

As I sat on a bench watching the Campus Corner Breakfast Nook, the squeaky-voiced woman with the freckles walked over to me with her strange mechanical gait. She asked some vacuous question, and I said, "You're a grifter. You should give me my two dollars back."

"I own a business in town," she said. Her purse opened, her hand moved quickly, furtively, and there was no look of shame. She seemed proud to have been caught.

Then at the train station, I met Paul Marie, the Amtrak host, a fat, toothless man who insisted that the train would take me to Montreal. I made it clear to him that I did not believe this, and I got his boss's card and photographed the station.

Paul Marie told me that the other crew were phantoms and sometimes would disappear for as long as an hour and forty-five minutes. I tried to get as much information from him as I could about the unit, the cars, the track, everything. I even talked to the conductor on the phone before the train arrived.

Once on the train, I changed clothes again, pulled down my hair, and tried to think in French. The wilderness outside the train was green, lush, and northern. Foliage flew by close up, but at a distance, old farmhouses stood still while we moved past. I knew the customs officials would board, and I suspected I might be turned back again.

When the train stopped at Rouses Station for the border check four inspectors came aboard and walked through the car. There were two women. One seemed rather brutish. She came on first and I watched her pace by. I didn't want to deal with her. There was also a thin one with severely pulled-back golden hair and the man who pushed me. He had a gray mop; sort of an early Beatle cut. They all spoke rapid French as well as English. I understood some. The bilingual game was a tricky one. I lied, saying that I hadn't been turned away from the border before. It was a decent lie but not effective. The man told me to get off the train.

As he walked me through the train cars to the club car, I asked him, "Would you mind if I took your picture? I'd like to have a keepsake for my scrapbook of the man who threw me off the train."
"No, that will not be possible," he said, his French accent making it somehow worse.

There was a small group of us taken off the train. We stood outside in a gravel driveway next to a small brown building with heavily shaded windows. Once we were off the train, I again asked the official, "Do you think we could ask someone to take a photo with my camera of the two of us shaking hands? I'd like to have a record for my scrapbook of the man who kept me from entering Canada."
"Not possible," he said again.

He and two women officials ushered me into a building. They put on latex gloves. They opened my luggage and searched everything. They asked me to open the lute case.

The man took me to a car and put me in the back seat while he got in the passenger side. A driver entered and they chatted in French all the way back to the highway where the U.S. Customs station was, in Champlain. I was right back where I had been a day and a half ago. As the car pulled up, first at the Canadian side, the immigration man said, "I wouldn't show up at the border again. Next time someone might rough you up."

Then he released me to an Amish cab driver in a broad straw hat. I got in the back of the cab. In the rearview mirror, I could see the driver's shaved upper lip, his bushy light brown beard, and wire glasses.

He took me back to America.

sky blue open

train tracks

stone in stream

gurgling chuckling chattering

chestnut rail ties

creosote odor

slept on covered stage

set up for later event

tent over eyes

hat helped

planning

walked out and

young women in

Italian trattoria

calzone!

no Pellegrino

drank something else

deserted morning street

instrument store

listened to elder's voice

teaching talking

student with mother

want to know?

on the knoll

light brown wooden
lute cradled on knees instrument
back well to round flab belly
neck angled left
hand tests
sounds of the wind
if I could tell
resonance how like
Homerian sirens
I do not know?
wooden rods spun
against glass vessels
haunting keening
but a lute plucked.

18

I WILL STOP AND PUT THEM OFF

I SAT IN THE sterile, institutional, green waiting area of the U.S. Customs station at the Canadian border called Champlain, after being turned back by the agents there for the second time in eighteen hours.

The U.S. officials put me on a bus going south right away because they thought I had been there the whole time.

The driver had dark skin and a British accent. He said it was okay for me to take my lute on board and set it on the empty seat next to me as long as the bus didn't get too crowded. As I boarded, I caught wind of a simmering argument between the driver and some of the other passengers. At first, I thought the problem was between two groups of passengers but then I realized the anger was directed at the driver.

A black man in a white canvas hat with a light-yellow bandanna at his throat and a dark-skinned woman with a very wide mouth were talking rapidly in French, gesturing angrily with open hands. Soon it was apparent that there were at least four passengers who were agitated. I overheard another man speaking sternly with interspersed Franglais, cautioning a woman traveling companion not to argue. I could not see these two. They were several seats in front of me. As the driver stepped on the throttle, he opened his microphone to speak to the passengers.

"If anyone disrupts the safety and security of this bus I will stop and put them off. I have the right to put anyone off the bus anywhere where there is a telephone." His English accent did not hide his attitude. He was angry but trying to restrain himself.

In an attempt to hide, I opened *Alias Grace* and read to myself, sometimes mouthing the words out loud in a low voice to help me stay focused. I was nearly finished with the book and was looking forward to *Lolita*. She was next. The women in these books kept me company, and I looked forward to their companionship. They kept me sane and secure on this journey.

As we got further away from the border, I began to feel better. When I had asked the Canadian Immigration official what to do to gain entry to Canada, he suggested I go to Washington, DC, to the Canadian Embassy. Fuck that. I didn't want to take the bus to DC. Instead, I began to figure out a revised itinerary. This planning was interrupted when the driver opened the microphone again.

"We will be stopping every two hours," he announced. "I need to have regular breaks. These are very strenuous driving conditions, and regulations say that drivers only can drive for six hours straight and must have a break every two hours. Where we stop there will be bathrooms, telephones, and vending machines. Do not stray far from the bus or I will leave without you. The break is ten minutes only.

"Now, you can see these driving conditions here, with the steep hills and the deep drop from the road . . .."

Out the window, I could see the Adirondack Mountains, with their forests of trees and stone outcroppings.

"If the bus were to go off the highway," he went on, "that guardrail would not stop it from tumbling and rolling. A car might be protected, but the weight and mass of the bus would be too much for any guardrail. I think you can understand that to be safe we must stop. These are Greyhound regulations, in place to protect you, the passengers. Your driver must be fresh. Beyond that, I retain the right to dismiss passengers who are disrupting the driver or other passengers."

I marveled at his frankness and the formality of it. Murmurs came from the rear seats, but the voices died out quickly. I was on edge. I heard someone say, "He shouldn't talk like that."

"Don't argue with him," said another voice.

I buried my nose in *Alias Grace*. These were the final chapters, called "The Tree of Paradise" after a quilting pattern, like each of the previous chapters. Grace had moved to New York and changed her name after her pardon. In this section, Atwood used Grace's first-person voice to describe her new home. A white farmhouse with shutters painted green. Grace was forty-five when she gained her freedom, noting while sitting on her verandah, that her menstrual cycle was three months delayed. She was quilting by herself in the final segment. I wondered if her farmhouse would ever become a tourist attraction like the place outside Toronto where the murders took place.

I felt a tremendous sense of satisfaction as I finished the novel that I'd begun reading in the Trenton facility. I now knew that I would not meet Margaret Atwood this summer, but at least I was one text closer to my Master's degree.

I reached for my cloth briefcase. Pulling the large zipper, I opened the green bag to see the folded pages of *Lolita*, like Lacey's fine legs, tucked up inside my Lands' End square-rigger. The book and papers undisturbed for months, all the paperwork for the bus and train trip, the information on lutes and music from the purchase. I had searched the Internet for Italian lute tablature. I longed for the company of a young woman. Meeting girls on the bus seemed possible, but with this smoldering conflict between the new immigrants and the bus driver, I suspected my latitude to engage others in gentle conversation might be severely curtailed.

The lute beside me lured my attention. I was tempted to look at the music book that came in the blue case. What harm would there be? I didn't want to open the case on the bus; fear took me and kept me still and rigid. Yes, I would be reading *Lolita* in a matter of hours. My oral exam for the Master's degree was scant months off and I had many books yet to read. In reflection, my focus drifted from the bag and the pages I held in my hand to the lush sylvan landscape. I had bicycled these mountains, through the Finger Lakes, as a teenager, camping and cycling many miles over mountain passes on two-lane roads. I had cycled through the Canadian landscape then, too. The big bus seemed stable as it curled along a ridge, the highway cutting across heights that had taken many days when I had cycled. I watched for hawks but saw occasional trios of buzzards circling on dihedral wings in updrafts waiting to feed on roadkill. The road kills were never visible. I could write a song for the lute about my adventures so far. Too difficult to focus. I wanted to take out the laptop here, but the battery would not last long and other passengers would notice.

I had read of the world of the psychiatric patient with compassion and become convinced that the doctor saw only part of the world Grace saw. I hoped I would figure out a way to get to Canada again someday. My relationships with Canadian friends were on my mind. The death of Mordecai Richler and bad timing had caused my friend in Toronto to suggest I postpone the trip. If only I had planned then to postpone the trip, I might have avoided rejection. Even my brother hadn't wanted me to visit. What could I learn from this trip? I kept replaying the border conflicts in my head and could not understand what had gone wrong. The first woman immigration official had taken an instant dislike to me. I wondered if perhaps Romanova, the young woman I'd helped to visit the states from Russia had betrayed me in some way to the Canadian officials. My thoughts ran in circles and went down rabbit holes. Riding this big gray dog toward Albany, I thought of my psychiatrist and realized how little he knew of my life. He was a pleasant older man, Czech, I think. He had worked in Oxford, Ohio for years. I needed to make an appointment to see him when I returned to Cincinnati. As for Carl, who knew? We'd been friends forever, but some part of me wanted more freedom from him. Having to see a monitor once a week was what was keeping me from getting closer to the young women in my life. I was sure of that.

19

Lacey #6

WHAT WAS I REALLY looking for? Lacey was young and her experience connected with mine only in little ways. I didn't expect her to want to be with me, but I desired her. I planned to read *Lolita.* Perhaps it would be the script for my connection with young Lacey. She had telephoned when I was in the facility in Trenton. It had been the first time we had ever talked on the phone. She wanted to drive up in her pick-up truck with Kerrie and rescue me. I tried to connect her to the social worker on my team, but it never developed. Counting on social workers to help with life was a long shot at best. From my experience, living life might just be too much for a social worker to understand. I wanted to live life.

I'd met Lacey's mother when Lacey was in Oregon. After buying Lacey a toe ring, I'd driven out River Road to New Richmond, where I'd found the Empress Chili and gone in for a meal. Lacey's gray VW Fox was in the parking lot with a "For Sale" sign in the window. Lacey's mom ran the place. She had red hair and cat-eye glasses, a ponytail, and a fine welcoming attitude. I asked her for Lacey's address. She gave me her phone number and told me to call her later on after work and she'd give me the address. When I got home there was a message from the clerk at the jewelry shop, saying she had found only one Montgomery in the New Richmond phone directory, talked to Lacey's father, and had gotten the address and sent the ring. I laughed out loud. I still called Lacey's mom to follow through and double-checked with the clerk the next day.

There had been the subdued conversation on the bus stop bench outside Sitwell's late at night, my right arm draped over her thin shoulders. She had listened patiently while I told her of the Memorial Day barbecue in the locked hospital. She laughed low at the description of sausages and grilled chicken breasts, without seasonings or sauces, single servings of Kool-Aid in Styrofoam cups, and potato salad with lots of Mayo but no onion. We had looked up together at the Esquire Theater marquee. Many of my friends had listened to me talk about the troubled times. Still, somehow, I was making Geodon work. Lacey had been a calming presence before I left for Vermont. As the bus rolled on, I was second-guessing the whole trip. Why had I left Cincinnati? Things there had been going so well compared to how they had gone in New York and Burlington. She'd asked me about LSD when we talked on the bench. I didn't know if she was experimenting or not. She mentioned her young poet friend in the blue velvet jacket. She'd wanted to sleep with him, but he was hardly interested. I wondered what was wrong with him without letting on to Lacey.

20

He Was Frozen in Time

I PULLED *LOLITA* OUT of the bag and rifled through it. Graduate students pronounced "Nabokov" one way and bookstore clerks another. It was okay for "a man of twenty-five to court a girl of sixteen but not a girl of twelve." What a thought. A man of forty-three could court a girl of twenty-five but not of sixteen, I imagined. Lacey was twenty-one. Well? I found this novel refreshing because I fancied it a bit taboo. I read Nabokov's brief sexual history of Virgil, Dante, and Petrarch. The narrator seemed to insist that any man who was a true poet needed to have sexual tastes that leaned to the extreme. Or at least to the young. Who was I to argue?

The bus rolled into a rest area. The driver was curt on the microphone saying, "Ten minutes only." I got off and found a vending machine where I bought M&Ms and a cola. I was in the midst of the tension as I stood in the green rest area with its concrete buildings on a hill overlooking the highway. The man in the canvas hat and yellow scarf was talking rapidly in French to his female companion. The driver talked to a small cluster of passengers, then walked away abruptly. The depth of all that had happened in the last several days flowed through me as if it were electricity. I trembled as I pulled the candy packet open and reboarded the bus. I'd been turned back from Canada. My brother would not speak to me. I'd left Cincinnati when

Lacey was giving me bedroom eyes and blowing me kisses. Now, without the grandeur of my train ride through Montreal and Toronto, I was on this Greyhound with these tensions.

Once we swung back out onto the highway, I felt some of the tension ease. I tried to focus on Humbert's imagination as Nabokov prepared me for another kind of love affair. The passengers talked in low voices; most of their anger seemed gone. I believed that I would be able to find a place to stay and get a shower in Albany. From there, I would cross New York State and head for Pennsylvania. This was to be my adventure. I thought about what was next and I could imagine many possibilities. Nabokov used erotic French words. Wouldn't it have been fabulous to be in Montreal about now? Humbert approached young prostitutes in Paris near the Madeleine, ahh Monique. I was too weak-willed to take advantage of a girl in that way. And I was not near the Madeleine, nor even in Montreal. I had chosen marriage some years ago and now was divorced. Headed on a long wandering ride back to my chaste home of Cincinnati where I must keep a certain decorum. A graduate student. That is what I must keep in mind. I wanted *Lolita* to leap off the page. I wanted to be in pictures. I was losing my big round belly as I became more active. Nabokov had me chuckling and thinking. The depth of his intellect was stirring. He had been born at the turn of the twentieth century in St. Petersburg. My grandfather had fled Russia with his family before the Bolshevik Revolution. They were born the same year. I felt a curious kinship that melted into wonderful admiration. This crazy artist Nabokov could inspire the rest of my journey and it would get better. It must.

I gripped a pencil and circled words that I didn't know. Incarnadine, coccyx, iliac. As the bus bounced, the point of the pencil snapped. No problem. I had another pencil in my bag. I looked around and felt indifference to all the other passengers. I had no desire to converse. Nabokov played with the French language in a way that was beyond me yet held a level of wit that I envied. Who didn't envy such talent?

My feet scraped the footrest and I considered taking off my shoes for comfort. I glanced around again. No one was that casual. The lady across the aisle wore white leatherette sandals. I had been thrown off the train at the Canadian border. An angry immigration official had threatened me. Was it possible to be rejected from Canada? Hell, it had been easier to get into Russia. This was 2001. I was beginning to hate George W. Bush. He had to be responsible. Did Nabokov have political trouble? Was my travel difficulty because of my writings? I could not believe that I had been singled out for some political reason. I read of Humbert's break up with his Valeria, with whom he dallied. She lied about her age even on her passport! This kind of narrative was over-the-top yet fit the purpose so directly.

I sat back and closed my eyes. The bus disappeared except for the roar of the engine and the gentle movements from side to side, the jostling up and down. I must have fallen asleep. We were slowing in traffic, off the highway, in a city. We must be in Albany.

I gathered up my gear, got off the bus, blinking, and paused to rub my face. I had fallen asleep. Where was I going to stay? I first went to the ticket counter and bought a bus ticket to Pittsburgh by way of Binghamton. It didn't leave until the next afternoon at one.

I walked out of the station and scouted around the block. There was a motel. I went to the counter, registered for a room, went up the stairs, and let myself in. Never was a shower so welcome. After cleaning up, I lay back on the bed and fell asleep immediately.

In the morning I found the breakfast bar and had a decent meal. The clerk at the counter showed me a locked room where I could leave my luggage until the bus left. I walked around town. As I looked around, I had an odd idea. The buildings were of stone and mortar, very decorated architecture on sloping narrow then wide streets. It seemed as if Albany's buildings were the tops of New York City's buildings. I had this notion that I was in some kind of time warp, and Albany was going to be jacked up to skyscraper height after I left. I was in the city before the City, a celestial architect of the mind.

On one large street, I saw a man sleeping on a bench with a newspaper covering him. I walked up to him and only then realized he was not real, He was a metal sculpture, frozen in time, the newspaper dated 1987. I read some of the paper. The detail was incredible, you could actually read the stories of the day.

I walked down the street past him. Soon, the area got rougher, with older, dirtier, gas-guzzling cars. I turned back and came upon a huge arena for some sort of sports team. I couldn't think of any professional team from Albany. Maybe the arena was part of the construction that would be shifted to NYC after I left.

Further along, I found a copy place that had Internet access. I checked my email there. Nothing important. I read the latest news about the Tour de France. Lance Armstrong, the Texan, was well-positioned.

The weather was great for walking, so I continued to explore. On a corner up ahead, I saw an older woman with an umbrella at her side. I came up next to her as the light changed. She stood still. I looked again. She was also a sculpture. A woman across the street leaned over the shoulder of a woman who stood on the corner reading her wide-open newspaper. I walked towards them. The woman reading the paper waited for the other to finish. Then the woman behind stepped around the other. The woman with the newspaper was another sculpture! This was a weird city. What was real and what wasn't?

All my walking had left me hungry. I had passed a bagel shop earlier. I retraced my steps and found it again, then hiked down to the river, munching on my bagel sandwich.

A tugboat was docked down by the river walkway. As I watched the wind in the flag, I thought about jumping aboard. The tug was ship-shape with the dock lines in tight curls on deck. No crew or captain visible. The sky was cloudy; the wind blew down the channel. Nothing between me and the open seas but a few feet of water.

21

I Watched a Girl Dance

He had an uneven gait. His freckled bald head poked out from a large, dark, dirty olive sweatshirt. The wrinkles on his forehead accentuated his bulging eyes as he moved past me, outside a cinderblock building with glass-block windows up high and down low, and said, "Aloha." Inside, an eerie but natural light filled the room. There were pews and old-style video games, the kind for drivers and shooters. Upstairs was a white-and-black tile bathroom that was clean and felt very old. The building spoke of an era gone by when buses were the only method of coming and going. Binghamton was small enough, and the train didn't pass through.

My bus left at one a.m., and it wasn't even eight p.m. I found an aluminum locker built into the wall. All my gear fit, including the lute. I fed quarters into it and put the key in my pocket. As I was leaving the building, through the glass door I saw the hours posted plainly. It closed at nine p.m. It didn't register. It just didn't register.

I walked around the town a bit and ended up in a small sports bar. It had dark brown faux wood Formica tables, with steel and foam chairs. There were trivia games and TVs everywhere. The bartender served me water when I asked. I didn't want to hang out at this place for five hours. I knew there was a university in this town, so maybe I'd find a coffeehouse with Internet access.

A place to settle in and just hang out. I overheard a young woman who was wearing blue-jean overalls. She stood at the bar, showing sloping cleavage, with long, light brown hair and the outline of a substantial, red, and yellow tattoo going down her back, visible above the neckline of her scooped gray T-shirt.

"My car is wrecked, and I gotta get back to Boston to work. I had two hundred dollars till last night," she said into a cell phone.

This guy in his fifties with a round face took in her every word. He had a black leather driving cap. He lit a cigarette and offered me one.

"Do you live here?" I asked.

"Yep." He extended his arm with the packet.

"No thanks," I sipped my water.

"Passing through?"

I nodded.

"What brings you here?"

"Just traveling."

"Off for the summer? Are you a teacher?"

"Yes, just finishing graduate school. You?"

"I teach here."

"What level?"

"I teach in an alternative school. Special populations. It's a target school."

I wondered if he taught gifted kids or disabled kids. Probably both. I decided not to ask.

The girl got off the phone, paid her check with a hundred-dollar bill, folded all these small bills into her purse, and walked out. It was starting to rain. A flash of lightning lit the entranceway, thunder followed, and the young woman danced out into the middle of the street as the heavens cut loose.

"Excuse me," I said to the man.

I went outside and stood under the green awning, watching her dance in the rain. Her kinetic movement stirred a primitive delicacy. She swung her soaked hair around her head. Lips curled as droplets clung to her face. She shouted a loud, high-pitched, wordless sound three times, ending in a sort of song. Her arms glowed golden in the light. The leaves of a tree on the corner quivered, drops of rain struck them.

The rain stopped as suddenly as it had begun. I walked on the wet sidewalks, a new spring in my step, lighter after watching the young woman cut loose. I looked for a coffeehouse, walking past a high school in the fading light. On the grass was a concrete signpost holding a metal sign. I stopped for a minute to read it. Rod Serling, the creator of *The Twilight Zone*, had graduated from this high school.

As the light faded, I found a phone booth with a torn-up yellow pages. There was one coffeehouse listed, and it was on this main drag—from what I gathered about three-quarters of a mile away. I headed down the street, across a bridge over a dank misty green river.

A yellow building housed a decent-looking pawn shop. In the window was a small box, blue Gibson guitar. It looked like the kind of thing Robert Johnson might have used. The tag on it read $50. This was a crossroads if ever I saw one.

A quarter-mile further along, past several fast-food joints, I found the coffeehouse. It was more of a knick-knack and candle store than a coffeehouse. And it was closed. I headed back toward the direction I'd come from. On the other side of the fast-food places, there was this ethnic food place that attracted me because it was so gritty. There was a closed-circuit black-and-white TV monitor inside, and I saw myself on the screen as I ordered something spicy that I didn't want and couldn't possibly identify. I stood there by the cash register looking at myself. I think the owner of the place was Greek or Armenian. He gave me these doughy things with meat inside. I wasn't hungry, but I knew I had to eat, or I would never sleep.

It was drizzling outside. At least I was out of the rain. That was something. The TV monitor glowed above the counter, mocking me. The counter had a Plexiglas window above it, with a curved opening from which the man handed me the food. I tendered cash, then went and sat in a bright orange bolted-down Formica booth, my back to the door. Even from there, I could see the TV glow and a tiny dark image of me, hands moving over the brown paper sack of food in front of me. Something seemed wrong.

I waited till the drizzle stopped, then walked the streets rather aimlessly for an hour, back and forth, pacing and thinking. There was a shiftless lack of ease that had come over me with the darkness and intermittent rain. I wanted to be inside.

I went back to the bus station at eleven-thirty to get my gear and catch the bus. There were a couple of people outside the station. One was this man with a white plastic pen protector in his shirt pocket. He had black horn-rimmed glasses and a bad comb-over. An obvious loon. I tried the door to the station. Locked. This time, the meaning of the sign registered. Fuuuck! I was fucked!

Unless I could get to the locker and retrieve my things, I would have to stay the night. I went to the payphone under the cement eaves where the buses pulled up. On the back of my ticket was an eight hundred number to call for help. I called and waited while an automated voice told me to keep waiting. A woman's voice finally came on.

"Ma'am, I'm in Binghamton, New York, at the Greyhound station and I've locked my gear in a locker. My medication is in there. I didn't realize the door would be locked all night and I need my medication. I'm not supposed to skip any doses. This is an emergency."

"I'm sorry sir, but there's nothing I can do. I'm in Omaha, Nebraska. All I can do is take your complaint."

"Couldn't you call the local police here and tell them it's an emergency?"

"I don't even have that number."

"Ma'am, you don't understand. Without that medication, I could have a very difficult time."

"Sir, there's nothing I can do."

"May I speak with your supervisor?"

"There's no supervisor here, sir."

"You're just alone in a room with a phone?"

"Sir, you can get your things in the morning when the station opens."

I hung up on her and walked back over to the bus stop.

"I'm going to a conference in Lancaster, Pennsylvania," the bald man said. "We'll be talking about the real problems and the real solutions."

I watched him pace and finger his dark blue tie.

"I've never traveled by bus before. Does this bus go on to Lancaster?" he asked me.

"I don't know," I said, "just check with the driver when the bus gets here." I walked back towards the bar.

When I got back near the bar, I saw another entry to a lower-level bar across the street. I went down the stairs. It was like a movie set, the way the bricked-in stairs led to a heavy door that opened into a low-ceilinged set of rooms with empty pool tables in partitioned areas, each dark partition with shelves for setting drinks. Antique beer signs hung on the partitions. The place was quiet. One couple sat together in a far partition. It was the rain girl and the leather cap guy. They had hooked up. I suppressed a giggle.

At the bar, a young, muscled and mustached tender asked what I needed. He wore a white short-sleeved shirt and black slacks. I had grapefruit juice.

"Is there ever any live music in this town?"

"Not much," he said.

"I'm a musician. Are there any promoters? It seems like with all these bars, it'd only be natural to have a little live folk music going on here."

"It's not my place," he said, "the owner is out tonight, but if you want to leave a number?"

"My name's Steve Lansky, and I'm just passing through. I'm looking to get a room at a motel. If I could get booked for next weekend and make enough to cover expenses, I'd stay."

He did a double-take. "I worked at Lansky's in Manhattan."

"Named after Meyer Lansky?"

"Yeah. You related?"

"No. It's funny though. My great grandfather's name was Meyer Lansky, and my uncle was Ben Siegel, but neither of them was the one."

"I used to work the door, carry home three thousand dollars a night. I handled some money there."

"Like I said, I'm a musician."

"What do you play?"

"Guitar and harmonica."

"Write your own songs?"

"No. Mostly traditional folk blues." I finished my grapefruit juice. He walked over to some new customers, and I left.

After an hour of street wandering, just moseying here and there in the misty night, I walked into the business district. I found the courthouse and sat on the concrete steps. They were dry now. I knew the bars were all closed. I was dead tired. I sang a cappella:

> Let it rain, let it pour, let it rain a whole lot more,
> when I got them deep river blues.
>
> Let the wind blow right on, let the waves roll along,

when I got them deep river blues.

Got no one to cry for me, the fish all go out on a spree, when I got them deep river blues.

Let it rain, let it pour, let it rain a whole lot more, when I got them deep river blues.

I got a gal, she's my pal, she walks like a waterfowl, when I got those deep river blues.

Let it rain, let it pour, let it rain a whole lot more, let the wind blow right on, let the waves wash along, when I got them deep river blues.

When I get down to Muscle Shoals, times are better there I'm told, I'll get a boat and if she floats I'll go out, when I get them deep river blues.

Let it rain, let it pour, let it rain a whole lot more, let the waves wash along, let the wind roll right on, when I got those deep river blues.

If I die Lord bury me deep, down at the bottom of Bleecker Street, put a stone at my hands and feet, when I got them deep river blues.

Let it rain, let it pour, let it rain a whole lot more, when I got them deep river blues.

No one heard my song but me. I walked, exhausted to a Days Inn motel where I got a room for the night. Once in the room, I called my telephone back in Cincinnati to pick up messages. My friend Niki, the DJ at WNKU had her baby boy, Silas. Her voice on my machine lifted me from deep in the depths to a new place. A new child. Niki, a mother. Some things did make sense. I took a bath and went to sleep.

In the morning, I felt much better. My watch alarm woke me in time to get back to the bus station so that I could find out when my bus left. I walked into the creepy building. It seemed fresher in the morning light. I cleared the ticket counter, then went out to a fancy coffeehouse right around the corner. I had fruit, a bagel, coffee, and juice, and enjoyed a curbside table as Binghamton bustled with morning activity.

Sleep and a good breakfast had stolen the idea of buying the blue pawned guitar and trying to become a solo folk revivalist here in this backwater New York town. I was Scranton, Pennsylvania bound, then on to Harrisburg and, sometime later in the night, Pittsburgh.

22

BEYOND BINGHAMTON

WE CUT THROUGH SMALL towns in the Allegheny Mountains. The driver did not make any strange pronouncements, and I was warmed by the lack of conflict, confusion, and difficulty. I think that this region has a strong kinship with Kentucky, Southeastern Ohio, Tennessee, West Virginia, and Virginia. I believed I was passing through the Northern Appalachians. When I lived in the most urban part of Cincinnati, I was among the urban Appalachians. I began to claim that I was Urban Appalachian by assimilation.

My family transplanted to Ohio from each coast of the United States. Dad's family of Russian Jews lived in Boston, Massachusetts, and Mom's family of Greek immigrants lived in Berkeley, California. My dad's offbeat humor often led me to repeat what he'd said. They'd moved to Cincinnati to be far from both families. Neither of my parents felt close to their parents. For me, this has been an up and down battle. I think it is odd to think of relating to parents as a battle, but it has felt that way at times. They'd each told me on separate occasions, and, at times, together, that the night they first met, they'd agreed they wanted children with whom they could have adult relationships someday. According to Dad, that night Mom was blitzed on Mai Tais and he'd crashed the party.

Since my schizophrenia had first been diagnosed when I was nineteen, I'd had had periods of extreme conflict with my family, interspersed with periods of closeness and support (which is not to say that conflict was absent before the diagnosis). I think that anyone familiar with the disease knows it is a disease of understanding and affects the understanding of all those who come into contact with it. At the time of this bus trip, I was not feeling all that well understood. I realize, looking back, that I spent a lot of money and experienced adventures with varying degrees of personal alienation and isolation. Interspersed with the confusion were moments of clarity and insight. In some ways, I saw myself as a traveling social commentator.

I'd always loved travel, and ground transportation other than the automobile had been a way of being in touch with the land, the people, and the places that had helped form my identity. Place was a part of identity. Pennsylvania was a place that I hitchhiked across many times when I was a teenager, from Cincinnati to Boston and vice versa while I studied at Harvard. (My bones remembered the cold rainy Novembers for which I was not well prepared.) I left Harvard after a year to travel, write and live in California, and I never returned as a formal student, though I did return to visit.

Leaving Binghamton felt like such a lift. The town had been a big night, a long exhausting adventure. Immersed in it, I felt a sense of freedom and anger. My anger was politically directed. I had a sense that there was no place for me or those of my kind. I must say that my position and social status as a worker had been affected deeply by my disability. Work, marriage, family, had all been disrupted by my schizophrenia. But the government, good social services, and a diverse network of fabulous friends had allowed me to survive it. Still, for someone on the edge of active psychosis, traveling presented a challenge. I knew that every day of my life I needed to acknowledge my condition and accept treatment to keep peace with the illness.

As a young man, I dreamed big dreams, yet I know now that many of the most ambitious of those dreams will never come to fruition. I wonder what part of my life is fate, and what part my efforts and endeavors can affect? I was about to contact one of my oldest friends from childhood to visit him and his life and see if I could gain some perspective there.

I saw an exit to Cooperstown from the bus window. The Baseball Hall of Fame. In my crazier moments, I had dreamed of baseball stardom. This was a pure dream, as I had no talent for the sport, only my imagination. Earlier in the trip, I had passed the exit to Schenectady. Union College. I had a writer friend there who directed literary seminars in St. Petersburg, Russia, where I traveled as part of my studies for graduate school. One of the writers I met in St. Petersburg was the poet Liz Rosenberg.

One night, over dessert at a restaurant off the Nevsky Prospect, we'd talked about our relative disabilities (I won't reveal the exact nature of hers, except to say that we understood one another). She lived in Binghamton and taught there. I had looked her up in the phone book the night I was wandering the streets of Binghamton but hadn't dared call. She'd confessed, in a candid moment, that on account of her illness, she wasn't sure if having her son, now a teenager, had been fair to her husband and the boy. I told her I wanted to have children someday, and I thought she needed to accept her decision and honor it. I wonder now, looking back, what would have happened if I had called Liz and she'd been home, if she'd have recognized my state?

The alienation and fear I'd felt from the rejection at the Canadian border was now several days behind me. The bus moved steadily on a warm summer day. Time slowed down as the gray dog stopped every hour or so in little towns. Some of the passengers were leaving home for the first time, traveling to see a relative, visiting a big city for leisure, or leaving home to join up with something larger. In Scranton, people who were going on to Washington, DC, stayed on the bus. I shifted to the Harrisburg and Pittsburgh line.

I stepped out of the stale air-conditioned bus air into the sunlight, the cool clear Pennsylvania light. A candy bar and a soda seemed like the true light of the universe. Brief chatter from someone in a station. The view of legs bent at the knees, seated passengers, waiting for their gray bus to arrive. Round and squarish faces. Faces over outstretched arms greeting an arriving family member with a hug, a handshake, a smile, a tentative touch of an arm. An old light green metal vending machine, chrome pull handles with heavy clear plastic knobs. The simple joy of candy. Chocolate. Chuckles, gumdrops, Clark bars.

This flood of lust on the bus, streaking past small Pennsylvania towns, Schenectady, Union College, Penn State, the moods of young boys all around, leaving their rural homes for the first time to go to cities, colleges, teams, the military. I was a recruiter in my mind for lust, for lusty me, for Lolita inspired *me*. Headed across green wooded Northern Appalachia only to return to my urban Cincinnati coffeehouse, borrow a blue Papermate and scribble notes about what was past in the present.

My thoughts now though were projective rather than reminiscent—about Lacey, about the people I encountered, about the shoes, the clothing, the haircuts, and the shift from a more fracas-oriented Eastern urban than rural motif, shiny shoes turned into pale leather work boots, stylish greased short locks to buzz-cuts, a more Midwestern sensibility with farm kids, mining towns, shirts that had similar logos, still somewhat Eastern, but with lighter colors that spoke of community colleges, agricultural schools, then the Amish with hats, mustache-free beards, young women with hand-sewn dresses and bonnets tied under their chins.

Gradually black people disappeared. While they kept mostly to themselves, a Germanic language overheard from the Amish sounded different, a little guttural. The young people were sometimes without adult supervision, going from one town to another. The adult men might be a bit drunk, hiding a bottle from the driver on entering the bus, swigging as the ride continued. I saw this kind of anti-social behavior, the public drunkenness, the rude carriage as something taboo, worthy of scorn, while my own kind of social ideation was okay. My tolerance for this kind of thing was limited, but for the time being, I kept my thoughts to myself. I was alone. I'd had enough conflict.

An idea that developed out of some reading from the early seventies: I was enamored with Buddhist Economics, conceptual environmental awareness. I think it was Ivan Illich who argued that the most suitable motorized personal vehicle would not go faster than fifty miles an hour or so. It would haul an adequate payload and have room for three or four passengers, depending on the weather. The mid-seventies Honda wagons with four-cylinder engines captured some of this concept. The idea was that if infrastructure stayed simple, population-dense areas would build rapid transit, that is, light rail. For longer journeys, higher speed trains might be suitable.

America's love of the automobile developed rapidly with the oil era. My ambition was to own a Porsche Targa and drive an hour each way on the backroads where I had bicycled as a teenager in the Midwest. On weekends, in all seasons, with my spirited cycling pals, we'd done everything we could to get lost between Cincinnati and the Indiana border. This commute to Miami University for work would allow me to stay in Clifton, walk around my urban neighborhood, and teach at a university two days a week. This plan was in clear contradiction to the principles of my youth when I had lived in Over-the-Rhine, using Metro buses and a bicycle. The trade-off now would be a life rich in social interaction at the university, maybe meeting some co-eds, communal time with a roommate or a girlfriend, and travel adventure alone on the twice-weekly commute.

In my pre-diagnosis life I'd driven a black Chevy pick-up truck in East Palo Alto in the mid-70s and ridden my Follis bicycle, but the theft of the bicycle and a weed habit combined with Wild Turkey that saw me driving drunk at all hours of the day and night (by God's grace I'd never had a serious accident though I scared a few friends more than they deserved), had led to my current preference for travel by rail. Unfortunately, the trains in the belly of the country were limited. It's Amtrak. Or Amtrak. I didn't understand at first, but as I got into *Lolita*, the book turned out to be largely about automobile travel, motel living, and the relative anonymity of such a nomadic life in the 1950s. Once the lust had been accepted, a certain decadence was implied, as was a new search for the poetic halcyon existence of a bygone mode of expression. The poetic fringe element had nothing on Humbert, the character, in terms of his conceptual high life. He was driven by lusts that, while admirable in a fifteenth-century European poet, might just be sleazy in 1950s Americana. In my dream, the girls weren't nymphettes, but they weren't my age either.

23

Afraid I'd Leave a Mark

I THOUGHT I SAW wheat fields in summer heat outside the window of the moving train. Moments earlier, I was in the Harrisburg train station on the long brown wooden pew, eating stale turkey sandwiches purchased at a small shop. I drank a bitter bottle of grapefruit juice. The terminal had a high, dark ceiling with an iron superstructure. A couple dressed for another time sat down near me and admired the blue case. I opened it, tested the strings, and lifted the instrument from the red felt lining. I always checked the tuning before lifting the lute; depressing the strings slightly to hear the clear tones. I played for a few minutes then stopped and put the lute away. When my train was announced, I walked down the ornamented wrought iron stairs from the open waiting area. This terminal felt large and small. It was larger inside than Pittsburgh. I didn't know that yet.

The train wasn't crowded, so I took a wide seat by a window and had another empty seat beside me. The back of the brown cloth seat directly in front of me had a gray folding tray table and there were black electric outlets under the window by the vent. I put the blue lute case above me on the luggage shelf, then walked around, found the roomy bathroom where I changed into shorts (I had been on the bus all day and it was warmer and stuffier on the train). As Harrisburg faded into memory, a conductor spoke on the public address system: "The Pennsylvania railroad had a Horseshoe Curve built to circumnavigate a mountain out of the Susquehanna River Valley. The Horseshoe Curve on the Pennsylvania line between Harrisburg and Pittsburgh was finished in the 1860s. It shortened the train trip across Pennsylvania from four days to a matter of hours. Before the curve was built, inclines were used to traverse the mountain." The view of the curve was dramatic; I had a sense that I was part of something larger. I could see other cars of the train because of the arc.

There were a few Amish people on the air-conditioned, silver train, the glimmer train where I later plugged my laptop in as night fell. I'd sent some stories and poems on the Internet to *Glimmer Train Magazine*. This was my reward. I never heard from the publisher, but here I was. Light pooled from the windows, gleaming, glowing, and making me want to move away from one side to the other. Because of the curves, I was always in the light. This train had a Midwestern energy. As the cars rocked gently through Central Pennsylvania, before darkness fell, more German-speaking men in straw hats with beards and no mustaches climbed aboard from small, exposed platforms.

The younger men were accompanied by cherry-cheeked lasses in bonnets. The children, boys in suspenders, girls in dark dresses, looked at me, their open faces inquisitive, warm blue eyes free of judgment. Their farms interested me because I knew they used limited technology, choosing to keep to older ways. The lute case, my old-style Macintosh laptop, the tattered brown rucksack, and my J. Peterman clothes kept me from slipping into the background. My white Panama hat shaded my eyes while I napped. As the train gently jostled to a stop, I woke enough to register this vision of another time.

I wanted to be here on this train that could be the movie train from *Alias Grace* even if it were a period piece from before the turn of the century. For the film I could be Dr. Simon Jordan, a psychiatrist, traveling from the Penitentiary at Kingston, Ontario to Toronto. The conductor's announcement of the Horseshoe Curve wouldn't fit the location, but it would fit the time period. I couldn't understand the script at this point. I wondered if this was a film of Atwood's book or some kind of updated version. I walked past people playing card games in the club car. A wooden phone booth. I dreamed this train. Who knew about my trip? And how many knew?

The film director would have to know. The crew would know they were shooting a film, filming the whole part, or part of the whole.

There was a virtual reality inside time. Time wouldn't matter exactly the same way in a filmmaker's mind as it would in an actor's mind. An actor would break the action into units and objectives. The filmmaker could edit the scenes. Essentially traveling back and forth in time but taking time to do that. Time taken learning a part would involve finding the right objectives. The whole film was always exploiting the writer's mind as he saw linearity and felt abstract emotion. Using time to draw a line between actors, emotion, with anima's knowledge of me as actor and writer. An act might hurt or heal a character. The scriptwriter would have to be on the film set, but only peripherally. He would be making observations, listening to the dialogue, watching dailies, and speaking with the director breaking down the action of the novelist's (my part) whose script he worked from. Kind of like shadowboxing, the schizophrenic follows three roles at once in his mind, and sometimes acts them out. The diseased mind doesn't separate the perceived actor, writer, and filmmaker, and might be all three but there is also a sense of a Higher Power, as director. When the Higher Power has been expressed through action then the time problem is not my problem. There were elements of prescience because life was not fair.

In Sitwell's Coffeehouse back home in Cincinnati, I could meet with friends. But now, now I was writing back story, trying to catch up with the action; a writer, maybe a physician, a psychiatrist, on a train trip; an anxious psychiatrist on a train writing down notes about some sort of reality, always shifting. (I did not take *Lolita* from my bag. I forgot the slender, elfin, downy-armed Lacey back home in Cincinnati. I thought about when I last saw her. She stood in front of Sitwell's Coffeehouse on the wide sidewalk, her back to the glass door. "Bite me!" she implored, offering her bare right arm, pixie blue eyes twinkling. I took her wrist in my hand, I held it, put my lips on her tender, tasty, zesty arm, half-kissing, half-biting. "Harder!" she said. I sunk my teeth into flesh; afraid I'd leave a mark. I could not hurt this smiling girl. When I stopped biting, she moved on. Now, I wondered if she had yet spotted Quilty?)

Life went on while I sat, eyes at the forward task of putting down words while listening to the gentle murmur of my thoughts. Was I writing the screenplay? Was I in it? Giving notes to others who were in it? Maybe I was just a graduate student on a train in a part of the world where some people dressed in clothes from another era and there was no mystery here at all.

I liked train travel. It was fruitful for the imagination. Planes were social pits. Driving alone was a marathon, full-scale combat with boredom and fatigue. Suppose it was 1861 in *Alias Grace*, and I was on my way to work in a psychiatric hospital in New Jersey. My writing was documentation of my observations. If I were to have any ethics, I must try the pills that I condoned. (In *Alias Grace* the prison was in Kingston, Ontario, and the hospital in Toronto where the trial was held. The psychiatrist had worked in other hospitals. This was in the dark ages of psychiatry before the miracle of medication. These elements of backstory were epistolary. In my story, the emails to make contact with Margaret Atwood formed an epistolary-like bridge. In my recent life, I was in a Trenton, New Jersey hospital, but I never saw signage to clarify for the film viewer what my experience might be if this was a film. I ate with the other patients, met with the psychiatric suits in their white lab coats with their clipboards.) I had been in other hospitals and worked in several. I knew the privilege of the keyholder. I saw the huddled psychotics begging for cigarettes and instant coffee. In one, as a public relations intern, I photographed a well-meaning Celtic band playing music for inmates. I'd been humbled by psychedelia and schizophrenia and chosen to pay forward my debt to medicine.

I had bicycle-camped to Kingston after my year at Harvard back in 1976. While traversing Ontario I had rebuilt my rear bicycle wheel at a public park by Lake Ontario after leaving Saranac Lake where I'd supported a team at the U.S.A. Olympic Trials for cycle racing. Cool-Gear Indy Exxon placed more cyclists on our team than any other at the trials. That year Dale Stetina made the team. Kingston had been the site of Olympic sailboat racing while I was there. Journaling about this had helped forge a budding writing career. I had sailed the Olympic class boat called a Finn on the Charles River in Cambridge while enrolled in college. Finns were cool because they had eight-inch halyards. To raise the sail, you tipped the boat at the dock, holding the mast until you could reach the steel shackle on the short cable while feeding the close-fitted sail up the mast. Then you let go of it, the boat righted, you grabbed the tiller, the sheet, lowered the knife-like centerboard, and off you went.

That long-ago summer in Kingston I met several Canadian students, drank beer, watched Bob Dylan in the film *Pat Garrett and Billy the Kid*, then cycled to Belleville with a fellow student I met in Kingston. We drank red-eye, tomato juice, and beer. I fell off my bike, I was so drunk. This real history was what I had wanted to parlay into a meeting with Margaret Atwood. I had stayed in Toronto with the Bakan family, psychologist friends of my father. One of the Canadians I met in Kingston was a photographer who had drying photos of scantily clad women hanging on a clothesline in his apartment. He had let me use his typewriter to chronicle my journey. My familiarity with Kingston, the friends there I had lost contact with, and my beer drunk with them, my drinking with the Bakans, one of whom had helped create Stepchild community radio in Cincinnati after he graduated Antioch, the denial that I had friends in Canada when asked at the border, which were the key elements of schizophrenia? Could I tell the difference between the good parts and the bad? Were there good parts? Was I just a drunk?

I walked to the club car, the train swayed beneath me, and I came upon a wooden payphone booth. We were approaching Pittsburgh. I went into the booth, fished some change out of my pocket, pulled out my little book, found Thad's number, dialed it.

Thad answered. I told him I would be in Pittsburgh at the train station in about three hours. He agreed to meet me.

At that time, I was listening to Bob Dylan's film soundtrack music. My teaching mentor, Dr. Tuma, back at Miami University performed Dylan covers on keyboard. I played harmonica. In my confused state, I was thinking that I was a doctor who had been given privileges in different facilities. But this train ride might replace that train ride for the *Alias Grace* film, and the train ride to Virginia might be part of a different story. Remember when the equine photographer mistook me for a physician? In my confusion, I was lying to him to cover up my anxiety about being a psychiatrist in modern society. Maybe I was like a psychiatrist, but I was a different kind. I accepted my role to help the ill but refused to play ball with the American

Medical Society. (Maybe since Harvard I could be anything I wanted as long as I took responsibility.) But then the whole experience started to look slightly twisted. I had all these things moving around me and I didn't track the primary focal point. For example, there were cameras monitoring most of the places I stayed.

No, I jumped off a train onto the tracks and couldn't explain it.

At the coffeehouse, there were "security cameras." In train stations, there might have been "security cameras." I knew they had them in Trenton State Hospital behind black, reflecting half-globes attached to the ceiling in the hallways. In the coffeehouse, there was background music, often roots music, including recorded work from Jake Speed and the Freddies among other local Cincinnati artists. On certain nights a Tarot card reader told fortunes. Just to be just to be. Ahh, I wanted out of these crazy fucking scenarios. I wanted to be on a train like back in the day when I played music and danced with young Lacey. And did I want to be a movie star? Known by one name?

I was into ethnic music, which had been an interest, and was part of the voodoo magic, a mesmerizing craze which went along with herbal cures, and then it melted into my story which paralleled the story of Grace Marks, and might actually have been the story, as I knew many mentally ill people and we took turns watching out for each other. (I was free to sit in public and work on my laptop anywhere. I have committed no major crime.) I was on the laptop, someone else was on the switch, someone else was on the harmonica. Hey, I may have typed my own, played through some kind of strange filter. Had my harmonica music been recorded without my knowledge? This paranoid fear surfaced here and there. I knew that I had figured out ways to put money aside and invest in research, and the public good. If my music helped others, then it was okay with me to share it. It may be that my music was part of the public domain. How did music relate to the illness? The Haldol tightened the digits of my hands. I played guitar and lute better without Haldol. Maybe harmonica better. Learning the lute allowed me to use polyphonic rhythms engaging my whole right hand. My hands were big for guitar fretboards. When I listed the effects of the medicine change, I told many people that my ear for music improved with the Geodon. I would not have bought the lute on Haldol.

Could I have lived and functioned in the community with the aid of Geodon? Could I have made this trip on Haldol? I didn't ask myself this question as I sat on the glimmer train. I never consciously thought I was on a train I had created out of my own mind. But before I was turned away from the Canadian border on the way to Montreal, I had hoped to meet Margaret Atwood in Toronto. I think this would have been true on Haldol or Geodon although it was unlikely, without being deluded, that I would have thought the lute might impress. I was an Exley of sorts, seeking glory through fandom.

In Atwood's novel, Grace remarked that she felt she was being watched through the keyhole of her room. I wondered if this was like the paranoia that I felt. When I saw cameras, I got uncomfortable. When I saw mirrors, I was usually okay. I knew that mirrors could be set up for photography, but I didn't think about that. The art and science of observation could be predatory as well as a necessary part of the healing process.

24

Pittsburgh–July 10, 2001

I HADN'T SEEN THAD since my divorce. A tall man with a dark beard, he and I had been buddies at Walnut Hills High School in the 1970s. It felt like I had walked in at a providential time. He told me that his wife was having alcohol problems. She was a stunning redhead, who wore gold jewelry to play tennis when they were courting. She was five-seven, a little rangy, had a good serve and volley. I knew him a little then, during his postdoc at the University of Cincinnati. He told me that they'd told the children just yesterday that they'd be divorcing. The synchronicity of this news coinciding with my visit scared me. Already separated from him, his wife lived a block and a half away. The children were traded back and forth. She was a lawyer who handled upper-class divorces that yielded her huge sums. He was an economics professor at Carnegie-Melon. His tenure had been refused so he was moving to the private sector, planning to create some software for hospitals with a mutual friend from Walnut Hills High School in Cincinnati. The friend, Danny, was flying in tomorrow from Minneapolis.

The next morning, I hiked across a splendid urban park in Allegheny County, near the Mexican War Streets. There was an aviary in the midst of the green space and diesel freight trains bisected the pond. A walking bridge over the tracks crossed a narrow road. I walked into an area built by the Carnegie legacy, found a small diner after watching workers bolting seats into the Steelers new stadium (there was a lot of black and gold). The Monongahela flowed into the Ohio. The diner, a Greek place, served a decent breakfast. I sat at the Formica counter next to a dark-skinned, well-muscled man with a shaved head. His wrists and arms were thick, as if he lifted weights regularly. He sported a small goatee, dark, business-like clothes, with a cell phone attached to his belt. He ate scrambled eggs with potatoes and white toast, and sipped tea. I had OJ, eggs over medium, wheat bread with a little butter, and potatoes with Heinz ketchup. We didn't talk. Something about sitting at a breakfast counter next to a black man felt uncomfortable. Cincinnati is the southernmost city north of the Mason-Dixon Line. In Cincinnati, breakfast counters were not so integrated. Yet, I felt good about sitting there, sitting with my discomfort, trying to think of something to say to the man seated beside me.

I had lost track of the beginning of the Geodon experiment, and had no concept of how it would end. I could experience Pittsburgh as a place where a friend who had left the confines of Cincinnati, and Clifton, had put down roots. This neighborhood near his home was much more integrated than Clifton in 2001. As I sat at the breakfast counter, I remembered the sensitivity training on race I went through for my social work job. It was taught by white men to white men and women. At the time, that had struck me as counterproductive. What could we learn about differences without embracing them? Now, at the counter, in reality, I felt good. Sitting next to a black man was no big deal, right? There was nothing to do here but quietly enjoy breakfast. Nothing to say. Was the Geodon experiment what brought me to Pittsburgh, to Thad, his wife and children? What was the story here? I was educated, white, mentally ill, becoming a post-graduate degreed professor. Trying to fill a need in myself. In the world. Looking back from the end of the Geodon experiment, this mid-story moment at the Greek diner seemed wonderfully innocent, quotidian, and serene. I remember it with peace, yet on leaving and reconnecting with Thad, my anxiety increased.

At lunchtime, Thad and I walked the dog, an eight-month beagle pup, named Scout, to Peppi's, a sub shop nearby. On our way, we bumped into a young woman from Walnut Hills High School in Cincinnati. She recognized Thad. She didn't seem to know any of our old friends. I named people and she shook her head, indicating non-recognition. I was impatient with her. This name game frustrated me, and I didn't understand why my friend was so patient and tolerant.

At the sub shop, I left him outside with the dog. I bought two Key Lime sodas and two Shady Side veggie subs. Standing, waiting at the wooden counter in the crowded, hot restaurant became a tremendous challenge. I wondered if my order was ever going to be ready. I wondered if I would go crazy, meltdown—right then and there—and I wondered if the short-order cook knew I was losing patience. My feet burned, and finally, I sat in a vacant booth to wait. There were signs about waiting and sitting, but I was so agitated that I couldn't determine if I was allowed to sit. Anxiety grew into fear.

Fortunately, before I could blow, my name was called, and after I got the sandwiches we walked to the park, sat in the grass eating. For dessert, we found a street vendor, Gus, who shaved ice by hand. He made us the world's best ice balls. This was living!

But then, out of nowhere, it started to rain. We got up and walked briskly, ducking into a Unitarian Church where Thad had a key. The mural in the church was memorable: bright colors, wholesome, unclothed figures dancing in the sea, a struggling boat edging away. In the church, Thad and I opened our sodas as we sat in a pew.

"She got aggressive. I don't know her anymore. Four nights a week at the bar on the corner. I can't leave the kids with her. The car crash was so scary. When I started going to Al-Anon eight months ago, it opened up a world. Other people. Understanding denial. At first, I got angry. Then I cried in the mornings when she wasn't there," he said. "When we told them, the youngest solemnly listened while the older one fidgeted and made faces."

I had heard enough. "After my divorce, I started going to meetings. It's only been a few years at the same meetings. I had training as a Chemical Dependency Counselor. You gotta find a spiritual solution. It's funny, growing up, you were the believer."

We were both looking at the people missing the boat in the mural.

"I guess I never knew," he said.

"I think of my Higher Power as a truthful force," I said.

We finished our sodas. "I wish there was something I could say that would help," I said.

"It's good. Good you were here now."

"I'm going to meet your youngest?"

"She's a pistol. It's the older one I worry about," he said.

After the rain let up, we went in Thad's convertible Saab to Carnegie Mellon to check out the campus. We climbed empty stairs wandering echo-filled hallways. My Harë Krishna devotee print hung in a frame on my friend's office wall. He confided that his colleagues and students asked if the drawing was a portrait of his wife and that his wife, "Hates that question."

I thought about how now we were both statistics, as folks say, part of the divorce culture, the breakdown of the nuclear family. In the trainings, I was taught that black culture, as well as poverty culture, often meant families of multiple generations lived together. Both Thad's parents were dead, as were his wife's. This would be a middle-class divorce. Thad would remarry and have another child.

We picked up his youngest at day camp. Thad told me that if he was late, he paid a fine. He chatted decisively on the phone with his wife using the headset. His daughter was happy, reading an *Archie* comic. We played a game, first to spot a VW bug, tags, no tag-backs, PT Cruisers, too. The three of us were laughing and smacking one another, tagging. We dropped her off with a friend who was rehabbing a row house. I had a hard time concentrating on what he said. We sat on the stoop and told jokes while the girl ate yogurt. Thad took me back to his house. He left to pick up his business partner from the airport. I snacked, carefully examining the food in the refrigerator. I had peanut butter on crackers and half a grapefruit. The food made me extremely self-conscious. I asked myself again and again what was safe to eat on Geodon?

I took a nap. While napping on the couch Thad's wife came in to use the exercise treadmill and woke me. Why didn't she work out outside? I clumsily, half-awake, stumbled down the carpeted stairs, ate a little more, answered a phone call, and then, sat on an overstuffed chair. I put a load of laundry in Thad's washer. He called and left a message. The machine picked up and I heard Thad explain that the flight from Minneapolis was canceled. I fell asleep in the armchair.

When Thad arrived a few minutes later, he scolded the pup dog for chewing a corner off the tongue of my shoe. I explained I didn't care as I had two pairs of the same shoes, one a size smaller, so now the larger pair was marked! The dog did me a favor.

Then we drove the convertible to the airport, wind in our hair, talking over the roar of the motor. We talked about drinking problems and came around to talking about God. My friend believed as a child. I was an atheist. Now, my friend wasn't sure he believed, despite his active participation in the church and Al-Anon. He was scared. I encouraged him to have faith. A sense of forgiveness fell over us. Danny's flight arrived and Thad called James Street to reserve a table for three.

At James Street, the Roger Humphries jazz jam was in progress. The jazz got hotter and hotter. There were three trumpet players in the septet anchored by the drummer. The band was all black. In Cincinnati, mixed-race jazz clubs were rare or nonexistent. Rod Stewart, dressed in a bright white blazer, white sneakers, jeans, wearing gold jewelry sat at the next table, his left foot tucked across his right knee. One trumpet was shiny, sharp, and loud. The player looked Eskimo, skin almost beige. A close-cropped Jeri cut covered his head. His forehead bulged. The bell of his horn seemed to always be pointed at me. He screeched, sputtered. When he soloed, his tongue trick was staccato as all hell. The keyboard player, loud at first, found balance as the horns gained. The second trumpeter had a bad finish on his ax. He danced. He wore a madras paisley shirt tucked into bright blue pants. Behind thick glasses, his eyes vibrated with intensity, as he tucked his knees together to get force. The bell angled up toward the ceiling. We sat at the best table in the bar. The third horn, an alto saxophone had a matte finish, but the sound blazed brightly. The man, dark-skinned with bug eyes, moved quickly and catlike, more than a bird, he pressed keys so evenly that the notes came in phrases and lines so proud and formed by breath, fingers, muscled sinew that I glowed in gratitude at having come from afar to hear these men.

The fourth horn was so strange. Called a fluglebone, it was a baritone trumpet or a miniature valve trombone with a squat bell, a tangle of tubing jutting below and left from his hands. The mouthpiece was larger than the others, the pedal tones were clear, enunciated, and perfectly pear-shaped, as if they entered the room with him, ahead of him, around us, and into us, a karmic, rhythmic issue formally blessing all who heard.

THE WORK SONG.

Roger kept time and was there, then gone, as if we knew time while he kept it, and yet it was there always, and not there, too. The bassman was big, black, and bulky, dressed in darkness with fast fingers timed to the keyboard, albeit imperfectly. The syncopation was in our heads and minds, then gone. The baritone trumpet wore a Miles Davis T-shirt; the first horn had a great floral with a black background. Only one man wore a hat and that was the light-skinned trumpeter, the tallest, with plastic-rimmed teardrop spectacles and a New York Yankees ballcap. This was probably the best jazz I have ever heard.

I played jazz trumpet in my high school jazz band. I remember the evenings in my attic room, finding the range and rhythm necessary to play a solo. Auditioning for the chance to play first chair (and winning). Here we were, in this crazy mixed-up new millennium, three Walnut Hills guys, a professor leaving academia, and a real worker, a mentally ill freeman, me, becoming solid enough to teach at a regular university to mainstream students. Ten years ago, this would not have been possible for me. What I didn't know then, and what I also didn't know at James Street, was that my job as a professor would require a lot of this kind of social activity when working with professors. I would come to travel in foreign nations where I didn't speak the language, and study with writers from around the globe. My horizons were just beginning.

We got back to Thad's home late, parked the convertible Saab in the alley. Inside I decided to call the bus station to get the schedule. A bus was leaving at five in the morning. I said goodbye to Thad. I took out the out-of-tune lute and played in the dark living room after everyone else was upstairs sleeping. I called a cab around four after writing this passage describing the jazz. My taxi turned out to be a PT Cruiser with GPS. I got to the bus station with minutes to spare, bought a ticket, and got on the crowded Greyhound with my blue lute case. Columbus came and went, then I was back in Cincinnati walking up Main Street with the blue lute case swinging in my hand.

PART 3

Bryant Ave
From porch 350 Middleton
Steven 9.29.20

25

DARK-EYED AMY

DURING THE SUMMER OF 2001, I saw one film seven times. The film was called *The Man Who Cried*, and prophetically I was the man who cried at the end every time. Each time I arrived at a different point in the film, sat in a different part of the theater, and watched in different screening rooms in the same theater complex, The Esquire, next door to the coffeehouse. I felt I was part of a film study group, but I did not meet a teacher. I was unguided. My interest was in the variability of perception based on where and from which angle the film was viewed. I believed that the main female character who spent the entire film trying to find her father was actually my daughter in real life. I thought she had made the film to reach out to me.

I tried to figure out why some scenes worked, and others didn't. I kept cutting in and cutting out. I was sure that some versions were different edits of the same film. But it was the film *Songcatcher* that had a different edit. (I was certain that I saw two different edits of this film on two separate occasions a week apart at the same theater complex.) It was like I had a busted heart. The Geodon was not working. There were explosions of lust and anger. Explosions of awareness of the reality of my lustful past just before I was first hospitalized. It had been a long time since I'd been with a girl. All those dark theaters with no belle companion. Dark-eyed Amy, my neighbor, living upstairs, blithely coming and going while I watched her and noted her Michigan blue parachute pants when she went for a run; or wearing a simple dress showing legs. I wanted to edit my view

of Amy so I could see her inside my apartment. I was afraid of
her relative youth.

When I was home in the apartment I thought of how cameras,
mirrors, lights, and microphones had proliferated in our society.
I could see lights outside the windows of my red brick house in
my neighbor's house. The filmmaker would steal ideas and share
ideas. There would be family secrets. That was why the book
would be of interest. Miracles did happen. Amy was a miracle
walking on the sidewalk or up the stone steps to the front door.
Sometimes I sat on the black iron porch chair and watched for
her.

At one point in the summer, I started pitching pennies from
one end of the porch to the other while waiting for Amy to
appear. I sat in the black iron rocking chair to rest my sore right
foot. I flung pennies the length of the porch across the tile floor
trying to pass them through the gap over the stone railing and
below the hanging roof. I had a juice glass made from a jam jar
and a plastic spare change cup full of pennies. I kept score to
track how many pennies I tossed off the porch in an hour (my
"pitch" count). Each time I tossed nine in a row I would drop
a penny in the juice glass. Every time a woman passed by the
house I would also drop a penny in the juice glass. I would count
up the total score when Amy returned from her run.

If I ran out of pennies, I'd collect all the pitches that never
left the porch. When I ran out completely, I hurried into the
house to find another cup of pennies from the back bedroom
and hoped I didn't miss Amy's return. By the time she returned
from her run, I was embarrassed by the game and out of pennies.
I ended up placing the juice glass on the tile floor of the porch,
trying to drop pennies into it from three feet above it. I figured
if I could drop nine in a row that would mean I had pitched a
perfect game. If a penny landed in the mouth of the glass then
bounced out, I would start over.

I had pitched two perfect games when Amy returned,
breathing hard and smiling.

"What a great run," she said, opening the door.

I said nothing.

26

Cycling Up Salem Road

Cycling up Salem Road from Kellogg—after crossing through Lunken Airport the morning before the weekend of the airshow, I started to put forth effort, increasing the tension in my legs and arms. A familiar feeling as I arced over the banked curve without tilting. The bank was all uphill and my pace was such that I had the middle of the single lane all to myself—and the machine was perfectly vertical. And then I reached up to adjust the blue, yellow, pink, and black, club adorned Colnago cap with a quick right hand, then flicked the brake/shift lever and downshifted, gazed up into the canopy of green trees above as my right foot pulled almost out of the old Shimano shoe. With a clumsy motion, I stretched against the strain of the hill and reached with my right hand to tighten the Velcro fastener on the shoe and made a hideous swishing sound as I swerved dangerously, nearly falling. The motion and sound combined to scare a squirrel, which with a snap fell thirty-five feet to the roadway with a branch under her. She scampered away.

I pedaled steadily, climbing to Wayside, past the early morning sprinklers, wide green lawns, Red Oak driveway lined on each side with stately trees. The roadway grew narrower, twisty, fell off on each side into gullies. I was wearing the Colnago hat I'd purchased with Mer when I bought the different-sized shoes.

I thought about Mer, her lovely face in profile, the eyeliner, and tiny wrinkles at the corner of her eye. She smiled in my memory of her. Then I turned left into Mike's driveway. I hadn't seen him in weeks. His wife's Westie ran out barking, and I hushed her.

I laid my bike in the yard, lifted the cover off the hot tub, and took off my shoes. The dewy grass wet my toes. Steam rose from the water. I peeled off my yellow jersey, my blue gloves, my shorts, and my underwear, slipped into the tub, and sighed with great pleasure. It was about six-fifteen in the morning. No lights were on in the house. Given that it was late summer, the sky was light. Dawn had come as I'd ridden out Kellogg some twenty minutes earlier. Dave, Mike's son, was out of school for the summer. I wondered if he'd awaken by the time I was ready to leave.

Mike knew about the med experiment. We'd talked beforehand, and yet there had been this long awkward pause on the phone last time we'd spoken. I'd told him of my plan to visit Rigo in Vermont, and then take the train to Montreal. He'd said, "Rigo is very angry." I didn't understand that then. Now I did. "He's been angry for a long time," Mike insisted.

I sat in the hot tub, put on the jets, and directed them at my sore knees, repositioning my body after a while to focus on my lower back. I was getting into better shape daily at this point. Doing the ride up Salem and Wayside was giving me confidence.

Thinking Mike's son Dave might be curious about the Mexican pesos I had in my jersey pockets, I'd also brought two golden-colored twenty centavo coins with pyramids, snakes, and other elaborate detail. When I'd been his age, I knew I would have found them fascinating. Dave had blue eyes, fair hair, and lots of curiosity. In his slope ceilinged attic room, he had maps of the Allies and Axis powers from WWII. He went to a Montessori school where he studied piano as well as history. I had given him his first spoonful of cough syrup when he was an infant. Mike had been working with him on baseball pitching. Dave was slight, and I thought he might make a great climber if he got into cycling. I didn't want to direct him, rather to attract, hence the early morning appearance by bike in his family hot tub. I wasn't sure Mike and his wife, Sal, would approve. But they tended to welcome me whenever and however I showed up. When I'd been going through my divorce a couple of years earlier, I'd stayed overnight in Dave's room while he was out of town with Sal.

Mike had invited me to join the Appalachian Writers group at one point. I liked to tell the story of how I had made him my teacher by having him step on my head. I told it whenever we were asked how we met. It never failed to embarrass Mike a bit and draw an uncomfortable laugh. Part of my way in the world was saying things that made folks a little uncomfortable. On Geodon, I think it came even easier. This particular morning, I was going for touching, meaningful and appropriate, never quite sure if I hit the mark.

I'd wanted to get a college degree in creative writing with an urban Appalachian prose writer, and I thought about what a piece of luck it was to have asked Mike to be my writing teacher in 1986 when he was courting Sal.

In 1998, when he and his family moved from Mt. Auburn to Mt. Washington, I helped with the moving party, and yeah, was off my meds then, too. Mike knew me as an adult as well as anyone else with the possible exceptions of my case manager, and my ex-wife. And he'd made it clear his house was my house—a kindness for which I was grateful.

My ex was an artist who turned away from painting and drawing to work with computers while I transitioned from social work to teaching, writing, drawing, and painting. Mike told me later that if she had reached out to him, he would have been there. The separation had been painful, had come during an unexpected medication hiatus. We were together for thirteen years, though only married for four, two of those separated. She biked with me but would have preferred horseback riding. When we finally split, she cut contact completely.

The sun warmed the yard and came up through the trees to the east of the house out by the street. A light came on in the upstairs bedroom, then one in the kitchen. I had been in the hot tub for twenty minutes. Mike came out the back door, said hi, and asked if I was going to stay for breakfast. "I have to leave for work in forty minutes," he said.

"Yeah, sure," I said. "Is Dave up?"

"He will be."

"I have something for him."

"Okay," Mike said. "You want coffee?"

"Sure. Do you have a towel I could borrow?"

"Hang on."

He ducked into the house like a deer into the forest. A moment later he stood on the porch, said, "Ready?" And as I climbed out of the hot tub, he tossed me a green towel.

Soon I was dried off and back in my cycling kit. My long hair, tied back in a ponytail, hung damp. When I went into the kitchen, the warm room with jars on shelves, knick-knacks, and bric-a-brac, my body relaxed utterly.

I wanted to tell Sal about being turned around at the border, about the time in Trenton, about how the whole summer had been such a pain, but Sal hadn't come down, and Mike was making blueberry pancakes and frying bacon on an iron skillet, and there seemed to be no way to tell my truth in this achingly wonderful kitchen.

I helped myself to a cup of coffee, found half-and-half in the fridge, pulling open the door carefully so as not to disturb the magnets and clips with postcards from Mike's daughters, pictures Dave had made, lists and photographs of Mike and Sal together on a boat.

I moved aside a newspaper, picked up a paperback of *King Lear*, and sat at the kitchen table by the door. Dave came in wearing socks, a T-shirt, and jeans.

"Hey, Dave," I said.

"Hey, Steve."

"Check these," I said and handed him the Mexican coins.

First, he hefted them a bit, then passed them from one hand to the other, clunking and clinking. After a minute of shaking them, he held them under the light over the table and examined them with increasing curiosity. He grinned, showed his straight white smile. At that moment I felt grateful for all the therapy I had endured and actually come to appreciate. Being part of Dave's life in this summer full of discomfort, ache, agony, trouble, angst, duplicity, and pain made me madly aware that I wanted someday to have children of my own, but not while my parents were still alive.

Mike flipped the sizzling bacon onto a plate with a paper towel to absorb the fat and then plated each of us a blueberry pancake. We passed around a bright tin can of maple syrup, eating in munching silence. The coins found their way onto the table. I relaxed.

"My mom has cancer," I said to Mike after Dave had eaten and put his plate in the dishwasher.

"Shit," Mike said.

"Yeah."

Silence followed. I finished my coffee, rose, and put my dishes in the dishwasher. When Dave had been a toddler and Mike and Sal had me and my then-girlfriend over for dinner in their Mt. Auburn house, I had done piles of dishes, pots, and pans by hand, and swept the second-floor kitchen while my ex read Dr. Seuss to Dave. He marveled at her smooth legs. Sal didn't shave. Memories of women, feelings of having left their care, and fear that my mother was dying swept through me, but I didn't have a clue how to talk about any of it. With my case manager, maybe, but not on Geodon. I needed to handle it. I had managed to get near enough to my friends to ask for help but didn't know how to ask.

I went outside, put on my blue gloves, the brightly colored Colnago hat, and my cycling shoes, then straddled the bike and pedaled out the gravel driveway. A light rain began to fall as I made my way through Mt. Washington to Beechmont and rode home through Mt. Lookout Square, Hyde Park, and Walnut Hills. Fifty minutes later, I coasted through Clifton back at Middleton Avenue.

27

Columbus Love Tap

I DROVE THE GRAY Toyota to Columbus at high speeds, revving the engine, keeping her in the power curve, passing left on I-71. It was a typical humid summer day, and I planned to see Columbus for the first time in years.

The rumors that all the development on High Street near where I had lived (Goodale Park, Victorian Village) was now an upscale bar and gallery district called Short North had reached Clifton in Cincinnati. I had been in Cowtown trying to get a CETA job in 1981 when there was one bar and one gallery. I passed Short North with the windows down, the sunroof open, and my hair blowing in the breeze.

I drove to the campus area and parked. Street Scene, the restaurant bar where I had binged after dropping out of Ohio State in 1982 was gone. Larry's Bar was still there with its green door. Larry's had a reputation as a gay bar, and the patrons liked that because it kept the riff-raff and frat boys away. I took money from the automatic teller. I used odd settings to take as much as I could; I wanted to take old ten-dollar bills. I was suspicious of the new twenties and they didn't have the new tens or fives yet. I maxed out my PNC card. Then I was walking down the street, with all this cash and these three thin black teens with Afro haircuts raced past on curb hoppers. One came so close that I reached out and tagged him on the back, saying, "That was close. You're it."

He stopped, gently laid the bike on the sidewalk. The other two kept on. Street Tough turned, said, "Touch me again like that motherfucker, I mess you up good, motherfucker." And he walked right up to me and with a quick open right hand tapped me hard on the chin. Then he turned, picked up his bike, and rode off. I was a bit stunned. My jaw stung. I walked back to my car. Cross Country Cycle and Ski, where I had worked in 1979, was gone, the yellow storefront partially boarded up right there on High Street. My labor had helped to build that business.

I remembered a conversation with Carl, my case manager, about Stephen Roach, the Cincinnati Police Officer who had shot and killed Timothy Thomas, an eighteen-year-old black youth in Over-the-Rhine on my birthday last April. That night I was with a young woman at an Irish Pub in Northern Kentucky. Jen, a lovely, lithe, musician friend had braided my hair while she drank dark beer. Later we had come back to my place in Clifton and talked into the wee hours of the morning. The next day there was civil unrest in Over-the-Rhine. These came to be known as the Cincinnati riots of 2001. After two days of them, the mayor declared a curfew.

Carl's wife was from Scotland, and her Uncle Sandy was a police officer there. Carl told me that he had asked his wife's uncle what he would do if a suspect ran away. (Timothy Thomas ran from Stephen Roach. When the officer caught up with the suspect in a dead-end alley, the officer shot and killed the young man, later claiming he'd thought Thomas was reaching for a gun tucked in his pants.) In Carl's account of Sandy's police method, he said if a suspect ran from him, he'd yell, "Stop." And if the suspect didn't stop, he'd yell, "Stop or I'll yell stop again!" We had laughed together over this in Carl's little meeting room on the twelfth floor of a PNC bank tower in Roselawn. I saw Carl for counseling weekly until I stopped making appointments. This was around the time I returned from Vermont. Carl had stopped by the house and left a note. He had called on the phone to leave messages. I left a message with the receptionist at Carl's office, "I got a gun and if Carl comes back I'll shoot him."

He had been in the habit of coming for home visits. On the last visit, I had asked Carl, "Are you going to kill me?" In the past when I was paranoid, Carl would always just say, "No." This time he hesitated, a grimace came over his face. He didn't answer the question. I said, "Leave. Leave now," forcefully. Carl had forgotten his umbrella in my hallway on a previous visit. This time he picked up his briefcase, got up from the navy, blue, futon couch after putting on his shoes, and then took the black umbrella from the hall before he left.

The thoughts I had after being slapped on the chin swam through my mind in swirls of dualities. I had won the fight by not fighting. The young man had blown up, lost his cool, while I had remained calm. But no, he had won because he had struck the only blow. Yet I did not go down. I was not hurt.

I rubbed my chin once I was in the car. I opened the sunroof. I wondered how the young man's hand felt. Doubtless, he'd told his friends a story after he caught up with them about how he'd humiliated this longhaired freak. In the aftermath, I kept all this to myself. No, maybe I told Carl. I would have to ask him if he remembered. I was glad the young man had picked up his bicycle and ridden away. I recalled many times how gently he had laid down the bicycle. He had not been hurried or reckless. The gesture was casual, purposeful, and swift. The bicycle had not made a sound when he let it go. He had not dropped it. I don't remember as clearly how he picked it up, but it did seem hurried by comparison. He was gone into the pedestrian traffic before I could register the blow. As I'd walked back to my car, I'd forced an angry laugh. It was a strikingly clear and cool summer day. Full of the energy of life, I'd driven home from Columbus.

I didn't plan to shoot Carl with a gun if he came by. I didn't have a gun. Gun ownership was not on my agenda, though I would admit that in my imagination a cowboy outfit with two holsters and matching pearl-handled Smith and Wesson seven shooters appealed to me. I wanted something different from anyone else's guns. Honestly, I doubted I could legally buy a gun, given my history. I knew I could buy one illegally, but I wouldn't. My idea was that Carl would come by the house, linger, ducking in the bushes till I ran outside and tagged him, saying, "You're it!" His blue-gray eyes would bulge behind his glasses, his mock fear would turn into a grin and giggle and he would run the other way, his big frame hunched over from laughter and I would chase him laughing and shouting. The thing that I kept feeling was a desire to have my own life. My own freedom. I think that being monitored worked on me in my paranoia and aggression.

28

Kelly and the Cigarette

Kelly was an old acquaintance. I'd first met her some years before when she was dating her husband. Before Sitwell's Coffeehouse opened, the same basement space was called the Cove. The Cove was a low-lit room with head-high small-paned windows lining the street-side wall. The decoration theme was nautical, and the place was under Tudor Court Apartments, a sprawling dark brick three-story complex that took up a block between Middleton Avenue and Whitfield Avenue. A lot of the apartments had small balconies. Because the apartments allowed pets, the rents were reasonable for students and working people. Dave, a husky, attractive young fellow bartended for the owner, and Kelly was sweet on him. Dave had a pierced tongue and moonlighted at a tattoo and piercing parlor. He rode a motorcycle and came from a large, tight-knit family of musicians, saloon and tavern workers.

I lived just a couple of blocks away from the Cove down Middleton in a red brick house with a tiled front porch. I had started going there more than a decade ago when I lived in urban Over-the-Rhine. I think my first introduction to the place was through a theater group I joined to workshop *Hard Nosed*. I ended up producing the play in the early nineties just as I was moving up to Clifton. The Cove had slow service, a variety of coffee drinks, a full bar, sandwiches, and desserts. It was a basement space, and not without cockroaches.

Kelly was a little stocky, with a pleasant face and an upturned nose. I was attracted to her. She had the dark eyes of a deeply emotional young woman and also talked while she smoked filtered cigarettes. She called me Citizen for the first few years of our acquaintance.

Later Dave opened the Comet, a two-room bar in Northside that had a great jukebox, which featured local bands including ones that played there regularly (The Fairmount Girls, Ass Ponys, The Comet Bluegrass All-Stars, to name a few). The kitchen was open till one a.m. nightly, serving fabulous San Francisco-style burritos with an especially good salsa of the month and jerk tofu. The Comet had simple steel furniture, some corner booths, and a good beer selection. Kelly partnered up with two other women and opened No Anchovies on Ludlow. This pizza place had the craziest looking pierced and tattooed employees, featured a mural of Ludlow's streetscape (which was later altered because, in the opinion of some of the businesses on the Avenue, it had political implications), and fabulous calzones. The pizza dough was tasty, the vegetarian menu desirable, and it did a steady business selling slices and whole pizza pies. The three women ran it for five years then sold the place. After a couple of years as an upscale restaurant called Silly Puddin', it folded (meanwhile the Cove became Sitwell's when Lisa took over), then Sitwell's moved into its current location in the shadow of No Anchovies as if Silly Puddin' had just been a place holder. When Lisa took over the Cove, she changed the decor to honor the British poet Edith Sitwell. She painted the floor yellow, replaced the tables and chairs with new ones that were a mix of different heights, sizes, and construction, giving the place instant atmosphere. She also somehow solved the cockroach problem, and hung leafy green plants in the street-side windows.

In my last few months of a nine-year run on WNKU radio, I recorded and aired my novel *Jack Acid*. No Anchovies and the Comet underwrote the production. I lost my position before the airing was complete, but that's a whole other story.

Let's come back to the present and recap for a moment. Lacey and Bart, this skinny bearded guy with long brown hair, who we jokingly called Jesus, started spending more time together.

Bart worked at Sitwell's after it relocated. One afternoon I saw them going to a movie. I asked if I could come along. Bart said, "Sure, but you probably won't want to sit with us because we'll be making out all through it."

I wanted very badly to be somewhere else at that moment—or someone else. From then on, I abandoned all hope with Lacey.

I was finishing my creative thesis for Miami University, working my way through a list of novels in preparation for my exam. Every morning I visited Sitwell's, book in hand. Usually, I would sit on the window seat on the blue cushion and have a breakfast of oatmeal with fruit. It had taken me a while to get through *The Naked and the Dead*. When I got to *Native Son*, the struggle about censorship in Cincinnati had reached another new milestone. I had written a letter about the issue to *CityBeat* newspaper. The Esquire Cinema owner had edited a film while I was in Trenton State Hospital.

When I returned, having seen the film's website, I wrote a letter that *CityBeat* published. In the meantime, *CityBeat's* film critic had been banned from the Esquire and many people stood in a queue to see movies while others leafleted the customers. The protesters were passing out nametags with the name of the banned critic. The line stretched past Sitwell's to the corner of Telford across from the ice cream parlor. This corner was where I had started performing on harmonica with Jake Speed and the Freddies. One night, when the line was long and Jake wasn't around, I borrowed a chair from the ice cream shop and sat on the corner reading *Native Son*.

I don't know exactly what my motivation was. It just happened. As I sat there, people stopped to watch, giggle, shuffle past. Some commented, "Should we tip you?" "Something about education?" "A strange protest."

After forty minutes or so, Kelly came by. She was smoking a cigarette and puffed close to me. "The Clifton Business Association is all up in arms about—"

In an aggressive moment, as a diehard nonsmoker, I asked her, "Could I have a hit off that?" She handed me the cigarette, which I promptly tossed on the sidewalk.

"Bad Citizen," she said. "How could you do that?" She picked up the smoke and strode off, cursing me.

The next morning, I was in Sitwell's seated at the nonsmoking counter when she came in.

"Citizen, are you taking your medication?"

"Okay, I know you're angry with me, but you were blowing smoke in my face."

"You asked me to come over."

"You came over and started blathering about the Business Council."

"Citizen, what you did was wrong."

I don't remember exactly where things went from there.

"Just because people get angry and disagree doesn't mean there's anything wrong with their medication. I don't think *you* should be medicated."

Kelly huffed away. Later, she apologized. I realize now that I was wrong in my action. But at that moment, I felt a big glow of heat in my head and my chest was tight with righteousness. It's impossible to know if I've reported this accurately. As the tensions in my life increased, my ability to report events became flawed. I recorded no notes of this particular incident but can say that when I was quitting smoking years ago, others often offered me cigarettes and I learned to break them in half and hand them back. This cured the others of offering me smokes. With Kelly, I had done nearly the rudest thing a person could do to a smoker. At the time, her reaction surprised me. I felt she was over-reacting. Now, I realize I had crossed a line.

29

BUYING THE LOOK

I'D ALWAYS WANTED A bicycle with all Campagnolo Nuovo Record parts. Made in Italy, these were universally known to sports cyclists as the finest parts made. Ever since I was a teenager, I'd been lusting for great bikes. Now, with my energy level up, my bank account relatively strong, the economy dropping, why not invest in something I knew something about, something that had lasting value, intrinsic value, something I could use and get tremendous pleasure from?

Was I thinking all this as I went downtown on an early August day? Hard to say. It's possible all these ideas came into play in fragments of consciousness. I know I was a bit scattered. I'd taken the bus downtown while wearing my boating shoes, which were terrible for walking on concrete. The Topsider moccasins were road-kill shoes. My brother had found one shoe at his daughter's daycare, and the other a quarter of a mile down the road on the double yellow line. When I'd visited him in the mid-nineties, he'd given them to me and they'd fit. Since then I'd had them re-soled and put in inserts pulled from an old pair of running shoes.

As I walked down Court Street on this hot, humid day, I had another mission as well: to get in touch with David Wecker, a Cincinnati Post reporter, whom I thought should be doing an article on civil unrest in Clifton. He and I had talked in the past, and after I'd recently witnessed what was being called an incidence of shoplifting, I wanted to know why the press hadn't covered it. Given the racial tensions in the city, I thought an instance where a merchant forcibly held down a black woman who was then arrested by police on Ludlow Avenue ought to be reported on in some fashion.

I'd dropped by the paper several times already and left messages at Wecker's desk. I'd also sent the Post a letter to the editor calling for George W. Bush to share the presidency equally with Al Gore, to make the election results more truly reflect the wants of the American people. I thought I'd mention this to Wecker as well.

To my surprise, Wecker was in this time but busy. He appeared to be working on some fluff article that struck me immediately as a waste of his considerable talent. He told me to come back later, and I assured him I would. I then walked down steamy Fifth St. to exchange some of the Canadian currency I was still holding after the aborted visit to Canada. At the international currency exchange counter, I exchanged the bills piecemeal in units of one hundred, one hundred, and fifty Canadian dollars. Even though the clerk was supposed to levy a surcharge per transaction, he didn't. I was suspicious of him for giving me a break, but said nothing.

By the time I had finished this task, walking block after block on hot, hard concrete on this humid summer day, watching the pigeons, the people, the sky above the city, Reliable Cycles at Vine and Court St. finally opened. I went in initially looking for a few parts and before I knew it, I was piece by piece, buying a pro racing bicycle.

Dealing with Gene, a man a little older than me, an active cyclist in his own right, whom I had known since the early eighties, brought me face-to-face with the business part of myself. Gene had a mustache, a workman's hands, a gentle smile, and a soft voice that worked into a shout when he was instructing his employees. He loved making a sale and had the Jewish pawnshop-owner reputation. In the past, I had not done much business with him, fearing I would be paying too much.

I'd met Gene one night, years ago, cycling back from Cleves on River Road without lights as it was getting dark. He had driven out for the Queen City Wheelmen's Tuesday Night Time Trial. I had ridden out from Over-the-Rhine, ridden the ten-mile time trial, and was making my way home. Gene pulled over, put my machine on his car roof rack, and dropped me off on Main St. in front of my apartment. He even had Gatorade in his car.

I looked at four different frames before deciding on the white, Bernard Hinault, Look frame. A French company that supported both Hinault's five Tour de France wins, and some of Greg LeMond's Tour efforts. I knew this to be a fine machine. (Gene had one of LeMond's autographed yellow jerseys in a frame up high by the door.) Much lighter than my Tommasini, the Look was also smaller. It was an eighties frame and I would set it up with parts from that period, though as near as possible state-of-the-art parts. This involved Gene going up and downstairs in his shop repeatedly, looking for just the right equipment.

I ended up standing on the hard floor in his shop for at least three hours, on and off, as the day progressed. He brought up brown cardboard boxes full of used equipment. After he had found a 175-millimeter Campagnolo Strada crankset, he could not find bottom bracket parts to match. He found Cinelli deep-drop handlebars and a long stem that were perfect, a nearly new set of Dural aluminum alloy, Nuovo Record derailleurs, front and rear, and shift levers made by Suntour Power Shifters, which mounted on the handlebar above the brake levers and were accessible from the drops or the upper position on the handlebar. I had never used that style shifter. My old bike had bar-end shifters, the spring-loaded Shimanos. The Tommasini had STI (Shimano Totally Integrated); the brake levers and the shift levers were the same. You pushed them sideways for shifting and pulled back for braking. That was the digital system that was the highest tech to date. Gene swore that the Suntour Power system was nearly as good and worth experiencing. I grinned with the thrill of having such a variety of top equipment. I even had a seven-block disc back wheel that a fellow had given me several years before that would fit the Look. Before we got to the brakes, Gene sent me away for lunch so that he could help some other customers.

I got some Mexican food on Court Street, then went back over to the Post. Wecker was available this time. He said he had to walk somewhere down Court Street, and I told him I was buying a bike at Reliable. We decided to walk and talk. He was six-four, well built, with a slightly pockmarked face, gray-brown hair, a fine smile, and a big firm handshake.

"I was ordering lunch at Burrito Joe's on Ludlow when I spotted an argument from across the street."

"When was this?"

"Two days ago."

"Okay, you were across the street."

"Yeah, you really should come up to Ludlow, and I could walk you through the whole thing."

"Tell me more."

"Well, there was a thirtyish dark-skinned black woman in a white tank-top and shorts grappling with the tall, European woman, Greta, who owns the Hansa Guild, a clothing and jewelry store. It's a cool store. Greta and her husband are in their fifties or sixties. She's a handsome woman who talks gently to her customers. At Hansa, they sell hats, woolens, and comfortable clothing, as well as earrings, pendants, and a small selection of rings. Greta and the woman were in the glass vestibule of the shop, and they were struggling. Then Greta's husband entered the vestibule from the store. He held the black woman. They were both shouting."

"You watched this from across the street."

Wecker and I walked past a parking lot.

"Yeah. She pulled up his shirt and scratched at his back. There was a lot of traffic going by, but I could hear them. A man in a suit and tie approached and handcuffed the woman. Then policemen started arriving from everywhere. A bicycle cop in a bright blue jersey was directing traffic around stopped squad cars. A bus blocked my view for a moment, but I saw Greta's husband hold his shirt up to show the red scratches to a male cop."

"It sounds like she was a shoplifter."

"I went back to Burrito Joe's and finished my lunch. When I was walking back to Sitwell's, I crossed the street and saw the arrested woman hustled, handcuffed, by a female cop out of a vacant storefront down the street by the library."

"I don't know, Steve. I don't think I can do anything with it. I'll let you know."

We were walking briskly down Court St. and I noticed that my right foot was hurting again. It had bothered me when I was tossing pennies, but now it was happening as I walked.

"Did you happen to see my wacky letter about time-sharing the Presidency?"

"I think so." Wecker walked a little faster than was comfortable for me.

"Bush being there for four years is so wrong given the popular vote went against him. I want to get a band together and tour Florida, see what the consciousness level is down there."

"You playing music?" he asked.

"For a while, I was playing with Jake Speed and the Freddies. I'm trying to put something together."

We arrived at the bike shop.

"See ya. Be careless."

His last words rang in my ears.

I went into the dark blue building, the shop with its clutter of cameras, stereos, clocks, instruments, jewelry, and bicycles. There was a remarkable, blown-up black-and-white photograph of workmen lunching on a girder while walking high steel in Manhattan.

Gene showed me some Modolo Speedy brakes. He said they were Italian Campy knockoffs and a lot cheaper than Campagnolo. I went for them. He found a seat post, a Cinelli leather-covered Unicanitor saddle, spare chain rings, Shimano clip-on pedals, handlebar wrap, a full cable set, and a Campagnolo headset. I left with a big burn mark on my credit card, a box of parts under one arm and the frame hooked over my shoulder. I caught a bus home, bubbling with excitement.

30

SMOKING IS ONLY ALLOWED IN THE BACK

EARLY AUGUST, EARLY AFTERNOON, sitting comfortably at a tall, dark, wood high-backed stool in the air-conditioned Sitwell's, drinking orange juice mixed with cranberry juice and lots of ice. Lisa, her blond curls curling with the humidity, was training a new employee. This was in the front bar area of the coffeehouse, a single large rectangular room. Smoking was only allowed in the darker partially curtained-off back area, designated with a sign: Smoking Lounge. The postcard racks displayed artsy cards featuring Man Ray, Mae West, Betty Page, Jackie Onassis, and all manner of odd bits of S&M, quirky nudes, pulp fiction covers, strange movie images, and carnival freaks. There were books about the Sitwell family on the counter, alongside a paneled pillar with photos of former baristas, regulars, and ne'er-do-wells. Among the books was a house copy of *An Evening with Edith*, a collection of creative writings by denizens of the place. The books were tucked behind a red gumball dispenser that offered seven chocolate-coated espresso beans for a quarter.

I'd just purchased a used racing bicycle in parts and spent the morning a mile up Clifton Avenue working on it at a bicycle shop owned by a high school friend, and now I was at the establishment of another high school friend, Lisa, the proprietor of Sitwell's Cafe. It had become my habit to enjoy my early mornings at Sitwell's after a vigorous walk there. I would ask Lisa for quarters to buy copies of the *Cincinnati Enquirer, The New York Times, and USA Today,* then sit at the counter with a pen, eating my oatmeal and fruit while critiquing the editorial content, layout, and design of the three papers, often exclaiming out loud when an article or advertisement was blatantly pushing a conservative agenda. I was especially alert to stories about violence by Cincinnati Police against black citizens. Lisa had been clipping articles for me while I was away, and I'd been working on an angry satire about blacks being sodomized by white Cincinnati Policemen. When new stories broke, I'd often use the computer terminal in the nook across from the counter to research the latest local news. The stories seemed to change rapidly as I came and went throughout the summer days.

In my more lucid moments I'd been discussing, or rather, holding forth (with anyone who would listen) on the idea of starting an alternative newspaper that would take a social justice perspective, employ young people as vendors and writers, and expound on local values and individuals. Some of the ideas were to address the police equipment down to the shoes of the different kinds of officers (mounted, desk, motorcycle, bicycle, foot patrol, and automobile). I wanted to know the maintenance schedules and performance requirements for the police cruisers. And I wanted to share human-interest stories on local amateur cyclists. The newspaper idea kept me happy and edgy.

I felt particularly good this day. A young blond fellow, well-built but more compact than me, walked in and took a seat at the bar. He ordered a beer.

"I've never seen you in here before," I said. "I'm Steve."

"Jason."

"You from Cincinnati?"

"Indiana." The barista brought him a bottle of dark beer.

"What do you do?"

"I'm a musician. I travel with a band."

"What instrument?"

"Percussion." Jason was smiling and drinking heartily. He had large deep green eyes, full features, and a warm smile.

"Really? A wandering gypsy? What sort of band?"

"We're called Homunculus."

"I've heard of you." I had read about them in *CityBeat*. "I don't think I've heard you play. Do you play a drumset? Do you have a CD?"

"We have two, and a third one, a live one, coming out soon. I play hand drums, congas, other percussion instruments."

"Any shows coming up?"

"The Mad Frog this weekend. We've also played York Street."

"Cool."

Jason was wearing a copper and brass bracelet. From where I sat, I could read the inscription: "Paragate Parasamgate Bodhi Svaha."

I asked him where he got it.

"My mom gave it to me."

"How old are you?"

"Twenty-four."

My mind was in a whirl. There had been an Indiana farm girl in Los Trancos Woods, California, twenty-five years ago. We had shared meditation, marijuana, and a passion for sex. I didn't want to deny the possibility. A flood of emotion pulsed through my temples. Was it possible that this young man was my son, and he had come here to meet me?

He finished his beer in a long swallow.

"Want another?"

"Yeah, sure."

"A beer for Jason," I said to the barista. "Drowning your sorrows?"

"There's a girl," he said.

"There's always a girl," I said.

The barista found the beer cooler in the corner.

He nodded and sipped the second beer.

I had been thinking about the rights and wrongs of buying drinks for friends and strangers, searching my morals because I no longer drank. I never knew if Julie got pregnant. But surely, I couldn't rule it out completely. She might not have told me. She had been twenty-six when I was nineteen. I left California. She could have returned to Indiana.

"How long have you been with Homunculus?"

"Two years."

"I'm thinking about putting together a band to tour in Florida."

"What do you play?"

"Harmonica and guitar."

Julie had worked in a bookstore.

"Is your mom into Eastern Religion?"

"She's cool." He looked wistful, stared at the liquor bottles and various drawings and photos of Edith Sitwell on the shelves behind the bar.

She had loved music. We'd seen Tanya Tucker open for Willie Nelson at the Circle Star in Redwood City. Tanya was only seventeen. The stage had rotated in the center of the huge round hall. The audience had been equally mixed between cowboys, boots and hats, string ties and all, and hippies with beads, long ponytails, girls in loose skirts. Julie drove a sixties blue VW bug. I remembered the authority she had in her hands, putting the car through the gears. I had missed the last half of the concert with a marijuana headache, sitting in the car out in the dark parking lot. Thinking wistfully about Julie, I remembered how well our young bodies had fit together. It had been a wild fling until her boyfriend came back into town.

Jason let on nothing. I was imagining the whole thing. Just because of the mantra I'd leapt away into all kinds of imagined stuff. Sure, she knew that mantra then. So did anyone who read mystical texts. She knew I went on Thursday morning walks in Golden Gate Park with the Theosophical Society. We had never walked together on one of those occasions. I must have just been getting further from my center.

A young blond walked in. She was wearing tight dark blue jeans and a white top that revealed her midriff, a pierced belly button, and shapely curved tummy. She stood at the bar for a minute, asked the barista for the manager. I overheard her tell Lisa about a film she was interning on.

"It's going to be shot in the Cincinnati area, and it stars Lynda Carter. You know, Wonder Woman?"

Lisa listened. "So?" she asked.

"Well, we're looking for restaurants to donate food for the production."

"Oh. I don't know. When will this be? How much food?" Lisa led the blond away from the bar. They sat in the middle of the coffeehouse.

I turned back to Jason.

"If I had a motorhome in Florida, and some other musicians, would you have any interest in traveling to play music? Maybe we'd fly down to Orlando."

He sipped his beer. "You're putting together a band to tour Florida?"

"Well, I'm just thinking someone has to go down there and find out what's going on with this presidential election farce."

Jason smiled again.

"I've just started researching on the Web, trying to find out what it would cost to rent a motorhome for about five people."

He nodded. "I might be interested. I've been thinking about branching out with some other bands."

"Once you're on the road, you'll forget about that girl."

"She came to my last show, but she left early. It's weird seeing her from on stage. Now, she doesn't answer my calls. I wish she hadn't come to the show at all."

The blond had finished talking with Lisa. She came over to the counter.

"What are you having?" I asked.

"That's okay," she said.

"Have a beer or a glass of wine. I'm buying."

"Well...I guess. I'm done working for today. But just one."

She sat down next to Jason.

"What's your name?"

"Stephanie," she said. She pulled her hair back from her face. Her eyes were brown, she had freckles, and her nose was turned up a bit.

"I'm Steve, and this is Jason. We're musicians. We're talking about touring in Florida."

"I'll have a dark cider," she said. The barista brought her a green bottle.

"Put hers on my tab, too," I said.

"Thank you, Steve."

"You're welcome, Stephanie. You sure you're old enough to drink?"

"I'm twenty-four."

"Where are you from?"

"California. But my mom was from New Jersey."

I had another moment. Jean, a girl I had met just before Julie, at a small street-side restaurant in Palo Alto, California had been from New Jersey. Jean and her thinner sister had worked at this Mexican Joint, and I had fallen for Jean. One crazy night the three of us met at a party on Middlefield Road where piles of green Sinsemilla lay in porcelain bowls and cigar boxes next to pewter trays holding cigarette papers. A belly dancer performed at the party, and Jean drank long-neck Lonestar beer. I remember that she nearly goaded me into a fight with a tall Texan in shit-kicking snakeskin boots by saying to me, "Are you calling my friend a liar?" When I critiqued an exaggeration of the other fellow. I said, "I'm not calling anyone a liar." She took me home to her waterbed after the cowboy tipped his hat and apologized to her. (The whole scene didn't make much sense to me at the time, as I was very stoned. I was thankful to have avoided a fistfight by grace.) We screwed each other into the night, and then I had left her abruptly; she cried and I lied and it was over. Now, I was freaking out quietly. This girl could be my daughter.

"I knew a Jersey girl in California many years ago," I said.

Stephanie looked over, raised her glass, and said, "To Jersey girls."

Jason lifted his bottle; I raised my juice glass. We drank, saying together, "To Jersey girls."

"So you're making a film?"

"I'm an intern. I just graduated from college, and this is my third shoot. It's a big film. Part of it will be shot in Toronto. Wonder Woman is in it."

"Do you have a camera?" I twirled my mustache.

"A still camera?"

"Yeah."

"Sure. I have a digital camera." She turned her head away for a moment.

"Did you go to film school?" I asked.

"Film was my Major. I went to I.U.," she said.

"Do you still live in Bloomington?" Jason asked as he rolled his shoulder.

"Do you want to go with us to Florida to document our tour?" I asked.

Jason laughed. I reflected a minute and watched the two of them begin to talk to one another. I wondered what would happen if they liked one another. It could be a problem if they were half brother and sister. Maybe they already knew and had planned this meeting?

Jason was finishing his second beer and trying to decide if he wanted another.

"That's it from me," I said.

I smelled cigarette smoke. I turned in my seat and saw the back of a thin woman sitting with Lock, one of the off-duty baristas. (Lock was a persona at Sitwell's. He was gay, always dressed in black with a black, short-brimmed cap, sideburns, and eye make-up. Often, he had sparkles on his cheeks and wore a pleasantly familiar perfume. Once he had displayed his artwork—dolls that resembled him in every detail, including studded necklaces, black leather wristbands, and belts with steel rings dangling.) The young woman sat at a round table in the front of the coffeehouse.

"Excuse me a moment," I said to Jason.

I stepped down from my bar seat and walked over to the table. These two were obviously eavesdropping on my conversation. The girl was wearing a top with thin shoulder straps. I put my hand on the bare part of her shoulder and said, "Ma'am, this is a non-smoking area. You are violating the law. I'm sure your friend knows this because he works here." She turned to meet my gaze with innocent eyes, and a rambunctious expression crossed her face.

I stared at Lock. I went right back to my seat. Lock and the woman got up and moved to the back. I was angry. Angry out of proportion to the gravity of the offense. In recent evenings, I had been regularly confronting smokers in the nonsmoking part of Sitwell's. It had occurred to me that some people were lighting up just to get my goat. If I'd thought about this, the karma of it would have given me pause. When I was a smoker, I often smoked in non-smoking areas and flaunted it.

Stephanie and Jason were talking and didn't seem to have noticed my absence.

"How did you get hooked up with this 'Wonder Woman' picture?" I asked.

She smiled. "She doesn't play Wonder Woman in the film."

"Oh," I pretended to be surprised.

"I worked on production for a couple of other films here in the area and I was listed with an agency."

"Do you know who's doing the music for the film?" Jason asked.

"No. I'm not involved in that part of the production. I could ask the director."

"Who's the director?" I asked.

"I'm not supposed to say," Stephanie said.

"A famous director?" I asked.

"Well." She sat silent, sipped her cider, and tossed her hair with her head.

"You ought to come see us play this weekend," Jason said.

"What's your band?"

"It's called Homunculus. We're playing the Mad Frog this weekend."

"What do you play?"

"Percussion."

I listened for a moment. My mind drifted. I felt incredible wealth. I had grown children who wanted to see their dad. Then the girl whom I had sent to smoking came back to pay her check at the counter. As she approached behind me, she said, "Hey, I want you to know I'm sorry"—

I cut her off. "You're not sorry, you would do anything you could to interrupt my conversation with these pleasant young people."

Jason and Stephanie turned and stared.

"You don't have any idea how selfish you are with your damn cigarette and your nasty attitude. It's like product placement the way you do that."

She held her pack of Marlboro Lights right in front of me.

"You're the nasty one," she said, "and you had no right to touch me."

"Hey, if you come in here you ought to wear clothes that don't show your tits. Wear a bra. You know better than to pick a fight with someone better than you"—I was shouting at her, and she shouted back, and suddenly Lisa was there between us. I jumped out of my seat, stepped into Lisa's face as she said, "Steve, get out. Get out now. You can't be putting your hands on my customers. You're making a scene!" And I could see Lisa's mascara and her wide blue eyes; her pointy face looking up at me with fear as big as the room. I thought to myself, yeah and everybody needs a scene for his or her stupid film.

"Well, here's my money. I'm down," I said, pulling my money clip from my pocket and peeling off a ten. I placed it on the bar and walked out.

"Don't come back," shouted Lisa.

I could feel the heat of anger shaking through me as I walked home. And suddenly my right foot hurt like hell. I'd been banned from Sitwell's. I wondered if I would ever see those two young people again. I was proud that I had taken such a strong stand against smoking, but by losing my temper, I'd set a poor example. Things had turned in a flash.

31

DARKE COUNTY DAYS

WHAT DID WE WANT to know about these local constabulary? We knew it was a small town. Steve knew he looked like a hippie to them. Steve looked like a hippie in a conservative gray sedan with a fancy bicycle roof rack. He wasn't sure if they were Indiana or Ohio. He was pretty sure they were Indiana and when he found out they were Ohio, it surprised him. The name Versailles sounded like Indiana to him. It was a name. It was dark. They couldn't see him at first. They knew it was a 1989 Toyota Camry with license plate ARJUNA.

He was out of the car after sirens and flashing blue and red lights, and a blinding white light in the rearview. He remembered driving away down a curvy country road, turning on his radio, loud to WLW 700 to see if these cops following him at all disturbed the conservative agenda.

He stopped. They told him to throw his keys out the window. He didn't comply. He got out, strode to the back of the car, facing all the white light. Expressionless face. Infrared targeting gun. He saw in the man's brown eyes and conservative brown flash of hair, the placing of a red X on his own forehead. He saw the flash of thought. *That is my X. It could be my eye. It could be my forehead.* He noted the man with the automatic pistol leveled at him in an offhand way. His stance and voice were manly. Steve was shouting at these men. He believed the main shouter commanding the "situation" was the man with the automatic pistol. Steve didn't know "command" as these men knew it. He was trying to observe through his fear, his trembling hands in their view. They wanted to see his hands; he heard that in their voices. He took command with his voice. Or tried to. He remembered the one who threatened with mace and ultimately put the cuffs on him and led him into the backseat of the patrol car. His face, the face of a man scared and abused. A grin of, "Hey you scared us you rascal, why'd you do that?" "You're not such a bad dude, hey?" And the blondish rake, the rounded forehead, the smile of near complicity, "That was kind of fun, huh?" All these things not spoken but interpreted off the glowing eyes and shiny white skin in the interior dome light of the not so sloppy, not so neat, deputy car. All the uniforms dark. It turned out to be Darke County, Ohio, where the MIA-POW flag flies just under the American banner at the jail.

I did not see the jail in daylight for several days.

My car was in a ditch. Off the road, nosed against a cornfield. I remember leaving it in the roadway. I cannot reconcile the view of my car from the back of the sheriff's sedan with my last memory of being inside it, walking around it to yell at the uniformed men. I had lost command.

One of the cars was a jeep wagon with a K-9 decal. I neither saw nor heard dogs, but I noted the detail. I'm pretty sure the K-9 man was the infrared guy. Why? I can't connect the inference. The faces disappeared after processing, became only memories. Who was at the arrest? I don't really have a count. I watched them pick through my car, trunk and all. They didn't seem to be methodical. Rather, I thought, they were disdainful, disgusted, a little put upon by the cocky rather tall gray-haired, brown-eyed contact and Khaki wearing hippie with the red sweater vest and sunburned shoulders, no belt, dirty white running shoes, and wool socks.

I don't know if I can tell you about Millicent, the Darke County lock-up, the fear of the wounded lion, the leg, the thirty-seven Tigers—the team that roared, the magic tooth, and the courtroom scene.

I can tell you that I was in the Darke County lock-up for a crime that appeared different from what it was. Yes, the deputies were sure I'd had a marijuana reaction, fled in my car after being awakened late at night on the roadside, and jettisoned the goods. They tossed the whole car and found nothing, not even a seed. So, when they ran me over stop sticks, flatted three tires, and created a crazy dramatic scene all they came upon as they came shouting up to my car was an un-stoned angry man. The facts? I was high on schizophrenia and my new medication, Geodon, which wasn't holding me at normal but letting me go go go. I thought I smelled marijuana, was sure fields were burning in the summer night in Indiana and Ohio, and it's possible I mentioned marijuana to the sheriffs. I had tried to close the air into the sedan and use air conditioning, but the internal conflict tugged at me. The four-cylinder engine had more authority without the A/C. I wanted to feel the breeze, smell the night air. The night was penetrated with dope. I believed that if I breathed outside, I would get high. In reality, it was the Geodon that would not stop my schizophrenic hallucinations.

Once I was in lock-up, this crazy fantasy began to develop to rationalize the whole scene to this middle-aged hippie. Millicent was a fair-haired man with elf-like features, whose brother had once been my closest friend. In Greenville, Ohio, where the Darke County lock-up was situated, Millicent and his brother had relatives. We'd always teased Nick in high school because he was nerdy and a computer geek. He was thin, lacked confidence, and had a soft girlish voice. His brother started calling Nick, "Millicent." I picked it up. But why had he come to mind? Well, I was in this building with a concrete floor and I imagined Nick had been there before. But not in the lock-up, in the area when the jail was built. It had pale green, painted steel doors with little wire-bound windows and I knew Millicent had set up his telescope on this very spot when the area was just a hillside. And further, I required, in my mind, that Millicent, in his own telepathic way, knowing that I was there, would come to do excavation and dig up this very cell because of some important insect fossil that must have only existed in this very region. And this would lead to my freedom and revenge against the Darke County lock-up and all its deputies. The jail would be reduced to steel and concrete rubble and salamanders would once again play under the rocks by the stream that watered the cows I could see from the window across from my cell. Though, now I'm getting ahead of the story.

So, I was the wounded lion. I knew eventually the deputies would get pissed enough at my behavior—trashing my pillows, tossing my toilet paper rolls in the sewer drain, under the grate, hiding my toothbrush, and generally being as difficult as imaginable—that they would beat me up. I *wanted* some of them to beat me up. I wanted them, yes, the deputies, to get pissed, lose control, and beat me up and I especially wanted the Corporal, Tom, to knock out my magic front tooth. Tom with the gray hair and mustache, the good gut, the jovial stern attitude. See, I had imagined that I needed dental work and as I had driven into Darke County after days of driving the highways of Ohio, I was sure that the main traffic on the roads was dental equipment. I don't have an explanation but truck after truck was designated dental equipment in my mind. Perhaps my madness was tooth aware in some odd sense.

I lost most of one of my front teeth in two childhood accidents, one on the playground in second grade at Clifton Elementary, and the other when I fell off my black, Huffy three-speed on Clifton Avenue a few years later as I was trying to make a big splash in a puddle and lost control. At the time of the bike accident, I was wearing Super Helmet Seven, a kid's toy helmet that had lights and beepers with seven different functions, a gift from my loving parents. Arriving at the dentist's, the road rash had made exiting from the car a stinging memory, but even more painful was the memory of many hours in the dentist's chair where all the work was done without Novocain.

I didn't get a permanent cap until I was in the mental hospital in Columbus, Ohio in my early twenties. On that occasion, I rode my bike to and from the surgery and saw framed newspaper articles about John Chamberlain, a Franklin County cyclist who had been a rival (not that he had noticed me), in Dr. Tootle's office. I never made the papers as a cycle racer. John had gone on to row crew at an Ivy League college. I had tried crew during my one year at Harvard but had given up.

Enough about the tooth. Suffice to say that like a wounded lion, I had prescient knowledge that the deputies would beat me, and Deputy Tom would knock the tooth out the old-fashioned way. My lawyer would appear, I would win the day in court and the press conference afterward, and going forward I would get better dentifrice. Every dentist since Tootle has said he didn't do a great fit. And the color is definitely off. All in all, I would be well served by the Darke County Dental Surgery and Deputy Sheriff lock-up.

Then there was the myth of the '37 Tigers. I imagined a great baseball team of bearded, longhaired, over-the-hill geezers who would stir the imagination of a generation. The Tigers would be the new team to play at the new park in Cincinnati after the war. I would come in after riding my Harley (or BMW) across Europe wearing a great brown bomber leather jacket and tear-drop shades. I'd take a ship across the pond and the train would bring me right onto the Cincinnati Stadium Plaza. The team would all come in individually. I would be the knuckleball pitcher. The off-speed stuff would flip out the adversaries. The game would be a live film set, and we would be the '37 Tigers. I think the '37 thing would be partly because the film would be set in 1937 and also because the youngest player on either team would be 37. Our opponents would be deputies and conservatives. The 1937 thing didn't fit with the war being over, but maybe I was thinking of a coming war or the Spanish Civil War. Sometimes my musings didn't fit right with history, as most people knew it.

Our team would be made up of the most outrageous PR men in Cincinnati. Heading up the Tigers haymaking effort would be ad-man and radio host, Jerry Galvin. His younger brother, Jene, would keep Cincinnati radio at a fever pitch about the game for years before and after it happened. I spent many hours listening to *The Stupid Galvin Brothers* radio show. Jerry's and Jene's voices echoed in my head while I sat in the cell. I could hear them working up a pitch. Anyone who knows anything about baseball in Cincinnati would appreciate the legs of this scam. It would outsell the '70s Big Red Machine. Finally, the Pete Rose debacle would be put to rest. The game would be all about racism. I would be the only white player on the starting Tigers. By the time the game was over, we would all be white geezers and we would still beat the reactionary players on the other team. The black players would win the day then be taken down for pinch runners, one by one. None of the replacements would be strategic, but eventually, the Tigers would be all bearded, longhaired men with baggy uniforms and high socks. The Tiger name would reflect the winning ways of the Bengals football team. Cincinnati would need more Tigers. There would also be some strange connection to Detroit that even I couldn't figure out.

I didn't know much about the other team, except that they would be embarrassed, they would lose, and the game would be seen all over the world by satellite and later by film in cinemas so it would create the first all-time baseball peace. For some reason that only I could imagine, this bunch of geezer Cincinnati players would capture the world's imagination. Countries would disarm to make the news during the seventh-inning stretch. The Tiger's slogan, "The team that roared" would be heard for generations.

Man, the jail cell was a wonderful place to cook up ideas. But being inside so much was difficult, and there was a little shame in shackles and striped clothing. I decided that Tom would not only be the man to take my tooth, but he would also manage the '37 Tigers. He was a good man, with a sense of humor and a breadth of experience dealing with people. He'd listen to the players and keep their individual personalities alive in the game. Jene would be in charge of infield chatter. I could hear him in my head now. Once I was shifted down the steel hallway with all the double-locking doors, unlocked with huge steel and brass skeleton keys, I recruited the whole team in my head. I had the positions filled. I knew that Tom was keeping me here for my leg. It looked now like they weren't angry enough to get the tooth this time. (My mentor, Keith, from Miami University had talked to Tom and explained that I went to graduate school and was on the wrong medication. When Keith talked to me on the phone in the processing room at the lock-up, he said, "Steve, they are looking for an excuse to beat the crap out of you. Just act passively. Be quiet, cooperative, and passive and you'll get out of there.") That meant there would be another visit to the Darke County lock-up. A visit for the dental work would be necessary. But my leg had to rehab. Yes, Tom the manager was resting me. I needed this forced rest.

I have to tell of how they took me, before they put me in striped clothes, to the courtroom. I was shackled hands and feet, with my hands in front of me. There were several prisoners, and we had to be tightly coordinated together, in shackles and side by side. I think some of the others were truly bad men. They seemed to appear out of nowhere as if they had been tossed through the walls with their guts, shoulder-length hair, pockmarked faces, crude tattoos, and indecent chatter. I kept my focus and did not look at them much. We rode in a van. I wore my crimson vest and khaki chinos. I had put a braid down the front of my long gray hair. Funny, but in both instances when I put the braid in, I went to court right afterward. I didn't know the first time that it would happen again, but it did. The braid was in the same place it had been the night Timothy Thomas died in Cincinnati. I had been braided that night by a young woman in a Kentucky restaurant bar. When I put in the braid, I thought of that very young woman. I imagined for a moment that I could have let them put me on Haldol, then they would have pulled me out of the jail and dashed me to a mental hospital. The van rode through Greenville's back streets. It pulled up behind the courthouse. I saw a TV camera and still cameras as I got out of the van. I smiled and looked into the lens. In the basement of the building, we were ushered into a small elevator. I saw a stairway across the hall. "I'm not handicapped," I said to the deputy. "I want to walk up the stairs."

The two deputies conferred, put a key in the elevator and one said, "Sorry, Steve. We can't do that."

In the courtroom, there was another TV camera. As we entered, someone handed me a little rectangle of paper. It was strange because, from the basement and hallway, it appeared to be a grand building with high tin ceilings, colored tile floors, and attractive railings, but in the courtroom, the walls had cheap fake wood paneling, low ceilings, and a general feel of the Sixties. I sensed that somehow this was another crazy set to fit the feel of the film that was being made. Here the cameras were on display. I decided that it was time to act. With the rectangle of paper, someone told me, "These are your rights." I was furious as I took in this stupid scene. The judge was a white-haired man with wire glasses and pink skin. His hands and face looked puffy. I was led to the front of the courtroom. He said something like; "Do you understand your rights? You may plead guilty, not guilty, or no contest." My hands were shackled to my waist. I held the little scrap of paper, crumpled it, and with a flick, by raising up on my toes and pivoting my hips, I tossed it onto the raised desk in front of the judge. "These are your rights," I said. Something else was said and I was taken away.

Outside the courtroom, they took me to a room off the hallway. I don't remember how we got there, but in this closet-like room, there was a camera and a microphone. I sat on the bench sideways, my feet propped in front of me, knees tucked up, and simply described the room fitting by fitting, board by board.

It looked like it had been hastily constructed. This was some silly film someone was making. I kept talking about the room. Then I said I was a thirteenth-degree blackbelt in Jujitsu. On the walk to the van, I had another photo taken. This was all before the Geodon was given to me. I felt agitated, angry, and confined.

Back in the cell, Corporal Tom told me that I was not going to get out soon. "You got the judge mad at you now," he said.

I think Josh, one of the other deputies, a tall man with a nearly shaved head and light blue eyes was laughing. I enjoyed it when Josh got a laugh. He had full lips that parted to show good teeth. After the shackles were off, and Josh was putting me in the cell, I asked him, "Josh, could I hold the key for a moment? I just want to know what it feels like."

He said, "No, Steve, I can't do that. Sorry."

"No hard feelings, Josh," I said.

I remember the flies, the breathing exercises, and Corporal Tom clapping hands. There were flies in the green cell with concrete walls. I sat on a steel bench upon a cushioned forest-green pad. Every so often, the bench made a clanging sound. It might have been doors banging down the hallway, but it seemed to me that the jolt was partially electric. I tried to sit on the cushion without letting the steel touch my body because I feared electrocution. They would drag my dead body out and I would be gone.

I lost faith in God and feared death for a moment, then relaxed and remembered that it was just a film. I would kill seven flies with one blow. I sat and breathed. I learned to draw in through my nose, hold the air, then push it out with pursed lips, a long white hiss of suggestion in the air. I could make them open doors with my breath. I could send different energies. I could blow people around with my grace. I did martial arts exercises to bring power into my willful gut. I tightened my grip on the individuals who could affect me. I talked out loud in French, trying to remember Victor Hugo's prison scene in *Les Miserables* from college French class. But I could not catch the flies in my hand. I could blow them out the door when it opened. Then I was taken to the processing room, seated on a steel and plastic chair across a gray desk from Corporal Tom. A Styrofoam cup of coffee sat near my right hand.

"You can have some coffee, Mr. Lansky, but don't spill it. It's hot."

I reached for the coffee, wrapped my hand around the cup, moved it ahead two inches, and put the cup down. I suppressed a laugh.

"Don't spill that, Lansky." Tom's eyes showed he wanted to laugh.

"Okay," I said. He sat back and as a fly flew up toward his head, he clapped his big, meaty red hands and the fly fell dead on the desk. He swept it off the top into his other hand and dropped it in a trashcan at his feet.

I took a sip of hot black coffee. I put the cup down, then pushed it with my fingertips.

"HEY! Don't play with that, Lansky," said Tom.

I laughed. The coffee moved in the cup.

Corporal Tom said, "Dr. Tuma is on the phone. He wants to talk to you." He handed me the phone. As I reached, another fly buzzed up toward him. He clapped and the fly fell dead.

I took the phone. "Steve, you have to be passive and cooperative and they'll let you out of there," said a familiar voice. "They're looking for any excuse to beat the crap out of you. I don't know what you did, but you pissed them off."

"Keith. It's good to hear your voice. It's a strange place to be," I said.

"I think they were going to let you go, then you pissed off the judge. Just cooperate, be nice, and try staying passive." His voice came through the phone in complete harmony with my breath. Keith's voice was distinct, scratchy, and breathy. I took his words to heart.

"Okay," I said. "I'd like to get out of here. Are they going to get me Geodon?"

"They're working on that, Steve. I don't know the details, but a doctor will see you. Just be passive."

We said goodbye and I handed the phone back to the Corporal. I picked up the coffee and drank it down, placing the empty cup on the desk.

"Tom," I said to this man who held my fate in his grip. "I'd like to get medication and Metamucil. It's very important that I get the Geodon in the morning about a half-an-hour after a meal. And I need Metamucil in the morning, too."

"We'll see, Steve," Tom said.

I stood there in my socks. By now I was wearing the green and white striped jail suit. It felt funny to be dressed this way, but I had written it off to wardrobe; it was just part of the role.

"Tom, you don't understand. I need the Geodon; twenty milligrams one time a day, preferably in the morning thirty minutes after breakfast. And I must have Metamucil. Otherwise, I'll get constipated and have painful hemorrhoids."

He listened. "We'll do the best we can."

When they took me back to my cell, a library cart came around with one of the older male deputies. I found the Big Book of *Alcoholics Anonymous*. I found a couple of paperbacks. I reacted less, stayed quiet, stopped singing, and meditated on Keith's advice. Yes. I must be passive. This would puzzle them, and they would cooperate with me. I had several conversations with Corporal Tom during which I repeated the request for Geodon and Metamucil, emphasizing that the timing was important. Then I started to read the rules of the place. The next day Corporal Tom used a high-tech scanning machine to record my fingerprints. He introduced me to Alyssa, whose code he used to activate the scanner. She had green eyes, pale pink lips, a little eyeliner, the deputy uni, and red hair sort of piled on top of her head with a few wispy strands framing her face. Her shoulders were wider than her hips, and her black boots shone in the fluorescent light. They moved me to another cell, off a room with a window, a TV, and a shower. I did exercises.

In the shower, I stood naked, my long hair streaming, wet and shiny. My body shivered in the cold water, my nipples were hard, and I rubbed the small bar of soap, quick like a fox under a waterfall. Afterward, I put on the jail clothing. The cell was only yards away and I could hear yelling. I passed another cell afterward and gave my minute attention to the young man under scrutiny like me.

The next morning a doctor came to see me in my cell. He was tall, like me, blond, with a short ponytail, and brown cowboy boots. We talked only for a moment. I asked him for Geodon. I remember the way he turned on his heel. I had the sense he was a horseman, maybe even a horse doctor.

Later that day, Tom came in wearing a T-shirt. I couldn't figure out why he was stripped down. He said the doctor was going to get my medication and he was going to personally see to it that I got Metamucil. I was overwhelmed with gratitude and relief. As I felt him warm up to me, I was able to read signs and papers that indicated it was proper to address the deputies as "Sir," or "Ma'am," or to call them by their last name from their name tags, and if they spoke to me and allowed it, I could call them by their first names. I spoke to each deputy I saw. Even if it was only when they brought meals, I spoke kindly. I asked for paper and pen. I found a phone book and made plans to find a tire shop in town and a towing service. I knew I could escape, get to my car and with my credit cards restore my car's running gear.

I also asked for the Ohio Revised Code, so that I could prepare for court. I studied the law. The charge "Fleeing and Eluding a Police Officer" did not seem to me a legitimate law. I was prepared to fight it on the evidence. I researched rules of evidence. I did not speed away from the police and I did not drive elusively. All I did was drive away and try to leave the town and county. I had done nothing wrong. The real crime was scaring people. I had not run away once I was stopped. I simply rejected the idea that I had to comply with whatever these officials told me to do.

Frankly, I had been more scared of them than they had a right to be of me. I had no weapon while they were packing all kinds of guns and back-up. They had trashed my car. I knew that once the whole thing reached court, the officers at the scene would be ridiculed, and the county would pay for all the new tires and other work. If I cooperated, I could get to court, and once in court, I could win the day.

I worked on contingency plans. I could plan for escape, recovering the car, or I could go through the courts and beat them that way. I requested maps of the county so I could develop a case explaining why I had stopped where I was parked. (Who knows what maps would reveal?)

Corporal Tom asked me, grinning, about my latest request. He did not fill it right away, nor address it in detail, just wanted to know what it was about. I told him that my lawyer would explain it when the time came. He frowned when I mentioned a lawyer. He said, sounding hurt, "If you work with us, we'll work with you."

On the fourth day, after being taken to the processing room I was given a blue and white Geodon capsule and Metamucil. I felt better immediately. That night I dreamed of Alyssa with the Breck-scented hair, puffed back, pulled above the ears, light mascara, gap in her front teeth. Just thinking about her I felt arousal. I remember my stiff dick. I could see her sitting on the bench, her legs spread, her hands struggling against mine, then holding on, and moving her butt forward on the green leather, parting her pussy, holding her above her waist with my right hand, my knees just below the edge of the metal bed, naked with her blouse pulled up, her teeth and breath on my cheek, kissing almost, then again, grunting.

"I love you, baby, I smell your breath, your pussy. My hair." Then I awoke with a start, stunned by the turn my unconscious mind had made into loving a jailer. The next morning Alyssa brought breakfast and I could not look her in the eye. When she came back to get the breakfast tray, I looked at her face, she took the tray, and with her left hand passed me a piece of paper with three words on it. I took the paper, read it, *They'll be behind,* it said. And I folded it in half, hid it in the *Big Book.* I had received the warning.

On the fifth day, I was taken to court again. This time I had a plan. They let me take a piece of paper with me for reference. I wrote down which Statutes from the Ohio Revised Code I wanted to reference. When the judge asked me for my plea, I would cite the passages on Rules of Evidence and Rights to a Jury Trial. They would have to let me go once I was on record sounding cogent.

As I heard the deputies coming in the door, I was putting a braid in the front of my hair. On the way to the shackling process, Corporal Tom chided me. "Now Steve," he said, "be polite to the judge."

I didn't say a word. I don't know why but I felt I had the upper hand. Josh was the escorting deputy, and by now, I believed his attitude was turning in my favor. The van snaked through the back streets. We pulled up behind the courthouse. There were no photographers this time. Inside, we were escorted to the elevator. There were only two other prisoners, and there were enough guards to keep us separate.

"I'm not handicapped," I said. "I want to walk up the stairs." We rode the elevator one floor then stopped. When the door opened a blond woman in a green dress and high heels climbed the marble staircase across from the elevator. "If she can walk those steps in high heels, I can do it in these slippers," I said.

"Well, this key ain't working right," Josh said, fumbling with the control panel in the elevator. He led me out the door.

I grinned and started up the stairs, the two tall, uniformed men right behind me. At the end of the second flight, I could hear them puffing. I had moved steadily, feeling the burn in my thighs. My breath was steady and quiet. They shuffled up to my sides and took me into the wood-paneled courtroom. The judge had not come in yet. The camera followed me. They took me to the front of the room. Then they played a videotape about rights and procedures. It was dumb and sad. American small-town justice. The judge came in. I stood.

He read the charges. "How do you plead?"

"No contest," I said. "I'd like to refer to Rules of Evidence in the Ohio Revised Code." I don't remember what pages and passages I cited, but I read them to the judge.

"I'll enter a plea of not guilty on your behalf."

I said nothing more.

He pounded his gavel and said, "Next case."

A bailiff escorted me out, and a reporter took my photograph. I saw Alyssa with the Breck scent in a yellow sweater and dark skirt. She stood in the hall, waved discreetly. As she turned away, I saw and heard her sucking a lollipop. Josh took me to the elevator, and soon I was back in the jail. "Why didn't you make a statement?" The Corporal asked.

"I said enough," I said.

The next morning, Tom came in early and told me I was being released on my own recognizance. In the processing room, he gave me a huge supply of Geodon purchased with the money from my billfold. He charged me for the pillows I damaged, then returned all my property. I got dressed. We discussed what would happen.

"Steve, you have to leave the county. Can you get your car running?"

"I have Triple-A and credit cards. I can call a wrecker, buy new tires, and I'll be fine."

"You'll have to pay $189 for the towing and impounding. In cash."

"Well, if there's a bank in town, I can get a cash advance on my credit card no problem. That's easy. Maybe if you let me call a wrecker, the driver can take me to the bank."

"That's okay, Steve. Josh can take you to the bank while I call Triple-A for you."

So, that's what happened. Josh kept me in the back of the patrol car. I felt like a VIP in the back without cuffs on. In the bank, Josh just stood there next to me. I got three hundred dollars.

Then they called Art at the garage. Art was the first black man I'd seen in Darke County. In his mid-forties, with inch-long dark hair tucked under a red and yellow trucker hat, he had a firm, rough handshake. He reached for a filtered cigarette as he put the rusty wrecker through the gears.

"The car has three flats," I said.

He drove to a warehouse-size garage and parked outside. "We have to switch wreckers to the big one," he said, leading me to the blue cab. I climbed into the truck. It roared as he flipped a garage door opener.

"We're going to meet the guy with the keys," he said.

Art drove to an intersection and pulled into a gas station. He smoked another cigarette.

"Do you know a good tire place?" I asked.

"Yeah," he said, "No problem."

A dusty Jeep pulled up and a blond woman with a tired expression got out and gave me my keys. "It's $189 for the impounding," she said after I shook her hand. I paid her the cash. Art followed the jeep to a fenced-in lot. She unlocked the gate. There was ARJUNA all wounded and sad. I checked for damage, examining the trunk. Although nothing was missing, it looked like someone had gone through my stuff. Art hoisted the car up onto the flatbed wrecker. He took me to a tire place, skillfully backing the truck up to the garage. I thanked him. Man, I love Triple-A.

I bought a full set of tires for around $200 with a road hazard warranty. Four men worked on the car at once as if I were making a NASCAR pit-stop. Two hubcaps were missing.

In Hamilton, I heard a scraping under the car and stopped. I found a wrench in my gray toolbox, crawled under the front of ARJUNA unbolted the plastic shielding that was partially detached, put it in the trunk, and wiped my hands with paper towels. Then I drove home to Cincinnati.

32

To Convince Even the Grebe and Goose

I WAS STILL SCARED of those knuckleheads. I dared not call them worse. I feared their absolute lack of mindfulness.

That summer I drove. I drove to Dayton, to Xenia, to Portsmouth, to Columbus, to Oxford, always on the backroads. I was graduating from graduate school. My time was my own. The car was paid off. The thesis was nearly complete. The reading list was under control. I was free to drive and live. Live life. I took morning walks, I stopped by the bike shop to turn a tool on my new Look frame, then I drove. (The steerer tube needed facing, and Glen let me use his Campagnolo toolset. I took down the cutting tools without his knowledge and worked on the bike quickly and securely. He got furious and threw me out of the shop. I walked it off. I apologized. He forgave me.) I drove to escape. I don't think it was a conscious choice always, it just got under my skin. I wore wool or cotton sweater vests without shirts. Sunroof open, windows down, I tanned my bare arms. My face turned reddish-brown. I turned to night driving after day driving. Long gray hair and dark beard were no longer marks of gentleness.

After the spell in the Darke County lock-up, I drove to Hueston Woods one night. I arrived at the lodge after eleven p.m. and rented a cottage. I drove the winding wooded lanes to the cottage, parked the car, looked around, checked out the rooms, then, flashlight in hand, hiked into the woods trying to find a lakeshore cottage from my dream. It had stone steps down to Acton Lake, a deck, a hot tub, all the amenities. I knew it was there. I was Dean of Students; therefore, my job was to let the undergrads fuck one another in the campground, while I found my secret cottage, reserved just for me. In the woods it got muddy. I strayed onto horse trails. I walked toward lower ground. The forest was dense. I hiked, holding my flashlight in my moving right hand, a natural movement of hand and light. Focusing the light only increased fear. The movement smoothed it, assuaged those scared feelings.

It was so good to be outdoors, to smell the muck, to hear the birds. I would single-handedly save a generation of waterfowl by scaring them into mass migration. I heard the ducks quack, the geese honk, the grouse grouse. Fall was coming; they needed to swoop south rather than circling. I could teach birds. I had a special skill to convince even the grebe and goose what they could not learn from the forest. Evolution had created me, the man of the hour. I was wearing my smaller pair of walking shoes without socks. I walked squishy into the lake. Cranberry bogs. These had to be cranberry bogs. I smelled the squishy loamy muck that oozed into my shoes. What a great feeling. Tepid water washed over my ankles, wetting the cuffs of my blue jeans.

I thought of Amy in the upstairs apartment. I imagined her naked. As I walked in the sandy, sultry wet mud, I remembered her comment the day after we met. "It's so hot up there I sit in my chair naked, reading." I told her, "It's cooler if you wear a thin T-shirt, your sweat causes it to wick, and with the fan on, your own sweat will keep you cool. I love to sweat." She didn't reply but hiked upstairs with my eyes enjoying a view of her shapely butt. She wore a plaid robe.

Then I was back in the bog, scared by a noise. I turned away from the lake and hiked up into the trees. The clearing now behind me, I swung the light up in a thicket onto a huge spider web pattern with a monster black and brown Wolf spider standing still in the light. My breath caught fear. I tasted my salty saliva. I stifled a shout. I turned away, ducked under some small branches, weaved through trees, making steady progress toward higher ground. As I stepped loudly, a bold white opossum, moving fast, paced by a foot away. It never slowed. I boogied with due deliberate speed, breaking out of the close branches to a trail, heart banging. Soon I was on a road. I heard animal noises behind, snarling, tooth and claw.

On the road, I was sure the satellites were monitoring me. My mission had been successful. Shadows of the tree line marked the edge of the road. I had moved the migration. I had saved the planet. I just had to get to the car. The road was long, dark, and winding. Undulating gently up and down it looked familiar in the cool night. After ten or fifteen minutes, I came to the side road where I remembered finding the cottage. I reached the car. I drove back to the lodge, returned the key, and drove back to Cincinnati with the windows and moon roof open. What a feeling. I was out of jail. I was liberated. When I got home, I took a bath and washed the grit out from between my toes. It felt so good to be muddy, to smell like loam.

Amy wasn't around, but I saw her darkness in my imagination, climbing up and down the stairs. She wanted to knock on my door again. One night she had come down and complained that her lights were out. I said, "Go down to the basement and find the circuit breakers." I heard her call a friend from her cell phone. I sneaked back into the bedroom and cracked the back door as she and this man walked, talking, down the basement stairs. I listened, but she never saw me. I lusted and hid.

The night came when I went to the Comet. I went to the bar, and the bartender, Patrick, a musician I knew who was in the Greenhornes, a local band, told me I had pushed him at a concert at Southgate House. I didn't remember at first. It came back to me as he described the scene. I apologized. He said he was angry, but he seemed to accept my apology. I decided not to stay at the Comet, the crowded, smoky, noisy bar. The jukebox was playing "Baby in a Jar," an Ass Ponys' song, when I cut out. I got in the gray Toyota. I would drive to Oxford the back way.

I cut through Northside and found West Fork Road, the mile and a half long hill through the backside of Mt. Airy Forest, a huge, wooded park in the middle of the city. I let the engine whine in second gear as I swerved around the tight corners. I crossed North Bend Road. This was the exact route I used as a teenager to cycle to New Baltimore, New Haven, Ross, and even Oxford. On Sunday mornings the Queen City Wheelmen, now the Queen City Wheels, a group of tough and ready cyclists of all ages, would race out these narrow country roads by rivers and farms. I swept through the suburbs and soon was on Harrison Pike. I drove in third gear and kept my hand on the high-beam switch. When there was no traffic, I clicked and lit up the road. I swung right onto East Miami River Road. Just as I came to the area where we had raced so hard in youthful, energetic competition, there was a giant hay bale in the right lane. I edged around it and slowed.

Around a bend, I saw the high headlights of a pick-up truck coming toward me. I flashed him my high beams. Something was thrown from the truck that struck my windshield on the passenger side shattering it into a spider web pattern. I smelled beer. The sound stunned me. Who would do such a thing? I slowed, flicked on the wipers, and came upon another hay bale in the right lane. I passed it carefully, ducked down, and stopped. I sat there for a minute or two, breathing and thinking. Someone didn't like me. Was it random or intended for me? Every car was suspect now. I drove slowly. I could feel my heart in my chest. My throat was dry. This was the worst yet, some kind of random, directly hostile act of violence. I could have been hurt. Why me?

I drove on, out into the country. I drove to avoid being noticed and worried that it would be a while before I could get off these country two-lane roads. I knew where I was, and how far I was from any help. My fear kept me from driving too fast, or too slow. I knew there would be drivers out here who would respond to a racer at night. I abandoned my idea of driving all the way to Oxford. I drove across the Miami River on the steel bottom bridge. In New Baltimore, I headed west for New Haven and Fernald. I drove the speed limit, vigilant for any abnormal following car. I saw nothing that indicated I was watched. I drove through New Haven and headed north until I got to Millville. There I backtracked into Hamilton, just behind a police car. Then I got on the new Highway 129 and sped past a Widmer's Dry Cleaner's van. Widmer's main location was in O'Bryanville across Madison Avenue from Chateau Pomije. I wondered what he was doing at this hour. I hit I-75 and drove in from there, speeding through traffic under amber sodium vapor lamps.

When I got home, I turned off the car, looked it over, and decided things were wild and I had better back off. But the other side of my mind was screaming, "Fuck those hateful bastards! I'm not going to be intimidated by anyone." I called the County

Highway Patrol and talked to someone who said I could make a report if I came into their station. I had had enough of police stations for a while, so I chose not to.

That night, I lay in bed a long time without sleeping.

33

L'Oiseau de Feu, Tom & Mickey

A LAZY MORNING ON Middleton Avenue where I'd lived for ten summers. Walking out the double entry, first from my apartment, then across the white carpet to the heavy leaded glass entry door, my bare feet first on the tired rope mat then onto the cold hexagonal tile, patterned after bathrooms all over this neighborhood. Identical tile to the bathroom floor on the second floor of the house I grew up in five blocks away. So lazy that I didn't have a newspaper, or a book, only a half-eaten turkey leg. I wasn't hungry for this smoked hunk of evil meat. I noticed Tom. Tom, tom, tom, tom. I laid the greasy meat and slack bone on the china floor. I looked up at the light-timed porch globe. It was late morning and the rusty tin mailbox had new junk. New junk! I was excited. Last night I'd danced the cane dance and sung of the great Pedro Archanjo. I leafed through the old torn *New York Times* in the green plastic box recycling bin. The obit of Jorge Amado. And not a single mention of *Tent of Miracles*. But for my new song, and me, Pedro Archanjo great hero of Amado's *Tent,* would be forgotten along with the story of Bahia. I'd sung: "Whether you sing in English, Russian or German, Pedro Archanjo is the greatest poet in all of Bahia. Dead or alive, Pedro Archanjo will be worth more than all of Brazil can—"

I'd been singing in the inner-city last night before my disc jockey friend, Nick, rode me home and gave me the greasy skin and bone. Evil meat. But the black and white spotted cat, Tom, the cat who, by his coloration would be Holstein (I think it's called a Tuxedo!), lay twitching his endless black and white tail on the gray wooden porch next door to me, and my bare feet, and my old yellow *New York Times*. Jorge Amado would be proud to have a writer of my caliber keeping time: tom, tom, tom. The tail at my foot. To the junk mail. A circular from the Cincinnati Symphony. Hope sprang eternal. Another season at Music Hall. The photographs, the names, the symphonies, Igor Stravinsky. I had once sketched him upside down learning from a book *Drawing on the Right Side of the Brain* by copying Picasso. *The Firebird Suite*, Stravinsky to be performed. "Tom, L'Oiseau de Feu!" I sang in a low whistle. "Tom, tom, tom, tom." Did anyone know that my destiny was tied up with a Corporal Tom of the Darke County Sheriff's Department?

"And what of Mickey?" I said aloud. "He's upstairs Tom! He wants L'Oiseau de feu! Too!" My upstairs neighbor had a brown and white dog named Mickey, a dog that I objected to at first, as I wasn't allowed canine pets, a dog that barked, a dog that tore up the yard. But Mickey would want the leg of the bird of fire! Could it be that the turkey is l'oiseau de feu? My invention. And would you believe that there was a judge in Kentucky, a musical judge in Campbell County, in Newport, where I was expected to appear on a charge of reckless driving in a day or two or three ... a famous judge, named Mickey? L'oiseau de feu between Mickey and Tom. These men both wanted my song of Pedro Archanjo, my song of great poetry, of English, Russian or German, my song of great worth? Should we say? Two men fighting over the leg of this writer, the turkey leg. Today, Tom and Mickey, today, I would ride my bicycle two hundred kilometers, and then Tom and Mickey, they could have—

"L'Oiseau de Feu, Tom, you may have it." And I dropped the greasy stump of the great bird into the bosh. Tom, tom, tom. Mickey will not take it from you.

34

White Wolf's Way

Yesterday I rode my bicycle two hundred kilometers. That's 124 miles. I went over to my friend Po's and asked him to go with me, but he said he couldn't, he had too much work to do (he does web design from home). I didn't always understand when my friends were too busy for me. I could get unreasonably pissed off. I didn't think I was showing how unreasonably pissed off just then, but maybe I was, because I could see Po was worried about me. At any rate, I left his place and drove out to Loveland on I-275, and when I got there I unracked my red Skycycle, put on my yellow bib and Colnago cap, and pedaled out to the beginning of the trail.

It was the perfect temperature, no more than eighty degrees, three-thirty in the afternoon on a gorgeous August day. I had no plan except to take a long ride to the north. I felt powerful and energetic in ways that I had never felt while on the Haldol. After a couple of hours of riding without a pause, I saw a herd of cattle, a pen full of wide-ranging snorting pigs, and crossed a great field. The sky opened up with the vista of the field, and joy spread throughout my body, a warm feeling of accomplishment. My breathing was steady, rhythmic, and mildly intoxicating. The longer I rode, the better I felt.

In 1975, on the summer solstice, I had ridden from Lima, Ohio, to Ann Arbor, Michigan, with fully loaded rack and panniers, a distance of over one hundred forty-five miles. That day had been brutally hot, windy, and torturous. By comparison, this was a picnic. But that day had been in daylight, finishing in darkness the final half an hour.

This time, I would ride for more than two hours in complete darkness without any lights. The moon helped, and when I was in open areas I could make out the trail ahead without difficulty. As I passed a hedge on the left a dog rushed out, barking loudly. I kicked to the side and yelled. I never saw the animal, but as my left leg straightened, I felt the calf tighten. The calf almost cramped, then released. I gripped the muscle hard with my left hand and squeezed, preventing the charley horse. Back in the toe-clip, I stretched, stood, stretched some more. I heard pigs grunting. Then I was motoring again.

When the trail passed into heavily wooded areas, there were times when I couldn't see the opening in front of me and rode right off the trail into the grass. I had to stop, put my feet down, and edge my way over, back to the paved part. At intersections, there were pylons in the middle of the path to keep riders from hitting each other when the trail was particularly crowded. The pylons were flexible, orange plastic on a spring-loaded base. I hit one hard. It scared me, and I worried more about damaging the machine than falling off and getting hurt. As the darkness became closer and more comforting my focus lapsed for moments and I lost a sense of where I was.

Then I felt twigs under my tires and a sapling whipped my left calf. In my paranoid mind, I thought it was an arrow shot by a protective archer, nearly missing me. I sped up. I passed a camping area that had a bonfire, heard people shouting, and worried that someone might be on the trail.

Once, I heard a voice and passed a man on a clunker pedaling slowly, appearing just before I was upon him, then just a voice again. Suddenly, I was back in Loveland as if I had never left. Tight muscles, a feeling of calm and accomplishment, a sense of peace sweeping through me.

It was nearly 11:45 p.m., and as I put the bike back on the roof rack, I realized I had cycled 124 miles in eight hours and fifteen minutes. Pleased and dehydrated, I drove to Kroger's in Loveland and with my credit card bought milk, bananas, sparkling water, fruit juice, and plums. I guzzled and gorged in the parking lot, then drove home.

The next day, I rode the bus downtown, sore as hell, dehydrated but needing to pay my bills. Years ago, when I lived in Columbus, Ohio, I wrote a bad check to a grocery store when I was on a bender, and when I got my life straightened out, I decided never to write another bad check again.

I had saving accounts and credit cards, but no checking account, and I paid all my bills by money order, buying them from Bob, the balding roly-poly teller at my local postal station with whom I had a love-hate relationship. Bob's money order machine was newfangled and often needed to be restarted by hand. I'd come in needing five or six money orders and push a couple of thousand dollars across the counter, and I could see Bob get visibly frustrated with me. But if I came in early in the day, to send a package or buy stamps, he was never red-faced, sweaty, or blustery.

On this particular day, for some reason, I went downtown instead, even though my bank was not downtown, and I did not need to take a bus to get to the post office to pay my bills. Nevertheless, I rode the bus downtown and stopped in at my favorite restaurant, Mullane's, and talked to the owner about having an art show there in the spring. She was very supportive. Then, in a rather unusual way, I borrowed one hundred dollars from her, so that I could open an account at a downtown bank that was offering better interest on saving accounts than my bank did. I don't remember the logic of borrowing from Audrey, but that's what I did. Then, without opening the new account, I got on the wrong bus back to Clifton, where I lived. The 19 Northgate bypassed the part of Northside where my car was being serviced, and I didn't realize until it was too late that I would miss my mechanic.

On the bus, I got into a conversation with a young woman who was lying to me. She told me her mother's name was White Wolf, and her mother taught at the University of Cincinnati. The young woman said she was a high school student. I asked her if it said, "White Wolf" on her mother's University I.D. She didn't know what to say. As I talked to her, I could feel that I was scaring her. I'm ashamed to say that I enjoyed that feeling. In my mind, I was teaching her a lesson. I don't think I taught her much, other than that longhaired freaky men on the bus can be scary. I told her that she shouldn't lie to strangers, especially about her mother.

After that, I decided to ride the bus way out to Northgate where I knew there was another branch of my bank. I needed to pay the bills by the next day at the latest, so if I couldn't pay them today, I at least needed to get money out to buy money orders so I could pay them tomorrow. I had the bills with me, so I could figure out the amounts. It was already getting near to closing time, and the bank was nearly an hour from my home. It was clear I wouldn't be seeing Bob today. I got there before closing and managed to get several thousand dollars from the bank without much trouble, though it took a lot of patience. Then I crossed the wide street to a T.G.I. Friday's and had a salmon dinner and a couple of cranberry and orange juices. I left my money on the table before I got the check and tried to use the Internet link in the restaurant because my computer at home was completely haywire. Then I left and started walking home. I had walked for a good half an hour when the car dealerships I was walking past began to affect me. I went from dealership to dealership looking to buy a car. I had ridden the bus downtown because my car was in the shop, and now I was looking at cars because I had ridden so far from home to this strip of highway where cars were bought and sold every day.

I spotted a black 1960 Studebaker, walked up to it, opened the hood, and saw that it had Mopar replacement parts.

As I think back on this now, some years later, it's as if it were the day these events happened. Here, paragraph by paragraph, alternating with a translation, is what I wrote in my journal that day:

> Been reviewing Alfred J. for the messenger service. Laundry detail mine again. Watching too much, I'm afraid, the messenger is confused. On the language block. Thomas Kemper visited an hour ago. Drank with him. Sat on the bench with a card in my hand. Think it was the two of clubs. Many days without wrangling. Señor Tané, cards on the table. Walls painted club colors. Pink and blue pictures in rooms with light curtains. Framing in France. Fumez veni? Cooking Lund with two secrets. Whisked with egg sauce, and used freeze butter (ghee) without burning my face off.

Translation: I'd been reading T.S. Eliot while doing my laundry. Thomas Kemper was a brand of root beer that I favored during this delusionary spell. I had printed out two different versions of two of my pieces of artwork and those were similar to copies of a van Gogh. (I had scanned the art into my computer.) I believed these computer copies were like the four aces in the deck of cards. Señor Tané was the title of both paintings. The mentions of the club referred to the symbol for Colnago bicycles, which was on my pink and blue cycling cap. That night after walking for hours, getting drenched in the rain and scaring the poor Studebaker salesman, I got home and cooked crepe-like pancakes from a Swedish mix of the brand "Lund."

The entry continues:

> Last four days hectic. France on fours. A lot of pushing. Drove a small red beetle through a rain forest. Geese are scared but turning North. Thomas Kemper grows cold at my feet. Cashed in on helmet law. Many wear them, mine rests, and I grow weary. Rise and fall. I hear rattling swords in the distance, reminds of when Thomas Kemper warmed to my hand. Firebird, Oiseau, and Tom sleeps on Daisy's temple steps. The big leg rests between two stairs. Tom is black with white ears, tips as if he had gray tomatoes. The sauce is so frum. Another sip please.

Translation: After I left the dealership with the Studebaker, flashing hundred-dollar bills and insulting the young black salesman who would not let me take a test drive, I ate at a Chinese buffet and hiked to a VW dealership where I test-drove a red Beetle. I did not wear a helmet on my bike ride. More silly references to root beer bottles. The Firebird was my nickname for the turkey leg I had tossed in the bushes for my neighbor, Daisy's cat, Tom. The big leg might also refer to my right leg, sore from the ride. I was enjoying the root beer and making up words to describe it.

And continuing:

Mopar parts difficult to get in frum sauce. Cattle tails flick. Studebaker has a new engine plan. Difficult to prove. Been on the table since 81.

Translation: I had some theory that most of the engine parts in the rebuilt 1960 Studebaker were manufactured in 1981. More:

Thinking ablutifitiously about starting a chess round about. Distance keys on long frapples. Drinking very clean and pure. Tastes spicy like alcohol. I think it has a red gram of vanilla and sarsaparilla candy cane. The frim fram sauce is better than cancer victim's sugar. Heard a little razz. Lumbering makes loud knocks. When the Studebaker door clicks open, then the back one sits, a wind break, the light side is how they shut, better than a rambler. As you say, one goes up the highway, the other comes down the path.

Translation: Here, I was imagining the ingredients in the root beer and expounding on my mother's cancer. I had ideas about how the Studebaker doors would latch and that it would be cool to drive with the back door open, a gangster leaning out, shooting back.

And the final bit:

The doctor left a message. If they's out a control, put a ham on the level playing field and call it a dashboard. A week from Friday, ten a.m. I practice volleyball with a friend.

Translation: I was making plans to see a psychiatrist, but all I had been able to do thus far was exchange messages with him (a long and relevant aside: The psychiatrist who had last prescribed my Geodon was the one at the county jail in Greenville. I had no scheduled appointment with my doctor at Miami University. I made an appointment with him and then canceled it. Then I tracked down a Buddhist psychiatrist whom I had seen when I was planning to go to graduate school. He had helped me with meds when I had been estranged from Carl, my case manager, because of my planned lawsuit against the doctor with whom he had worked back in 1998. That doctor had allowed me to reduce my medication—a whole story in itself. So, estranged from Carl, working with another therapist and this Buddhist doctor, I got into Miami without even connecting the fact that Carl had attended Miami. Once on the student health plan, I went to the counseling services and met a counselor and a doctor. This counselor encouraged me to reconnect with Carl.

The problem was with my divorce now final; I had lost my health benefits and could no longer afford the Buddhist. He said he had a daughter starting college and needed to charge $125 an hour, but I could pay with a credit card. Or I could see him every other week. He would not discuss medication on the phone. I asked what his daughter was studying. He said writing and art. I offered to tutor her for a discount or swap. He said no thanks. I made an appointment with him anyway. The day I had the blow-up at Sitwell's over the cigarette smoker was the day I forgot the first appointment. When I came home from Sitwell's, there was a message on my telephone answering machine from him. I called back and made a second appointment but missed that one, too).

Sitting in the open office off the Volkswagen showroom, I asked the VW dealer for a ride home. We'd been talking about engineering and the military, and I'd told him I was a graduate student at Miami University working on my thesis. When I asked him for a ride, he brushed it off, and we kept talking for a bit. I guess he still had ideas about selling me a car, but we were miles apart on price, and once it became clear no sale was happening, he lost interest, and I walked out and started walking down Colerain Avenue. By that time, it was after ten-thirty, and I hoped a bus would come. I kept hiking, feeling a need to stay kinetic. I walked over a mile before a bus pulled over for me. Next thing I knew, I was down in the West End on Dalton Street near the Main Post Office and the Metro Station. I stood with a security guard and caught a 31 Crosstown up to Hughes Corner, transferred to the 17, and got off on Ludlow. The whole time I was on the bus, I kept thinking about how much cash I had on me.

When I arrived home, there was a business card jammed in the doorframe. My old friend Betsy had stopped by. I had a lot of affection for her. She was a confident, self-possessed woman whom I had always wanted to date, but the timing had never been right. She was a few years older than me. The note on the back of her card asked me to call her when I got home, no matter what time. I was happy and hopeful at the prospect of seeing Betsy. The card listed her as a member of the Mobile Crisis Team. I called, got an answering service, and left a message; then, I went to sleep.

In the morning, I had some breakfast and started a load of laundry. I felt a bit dazed, sore, and dehydrated. The bike ride and all the walking had depleted my electrolytes, so I drank Gatorade, water, and juice. I took my morning medication and Metamucil. Just before noon, as I prepared to go to the Post Office to pay my bills, I got a call from Betsy. She was on Ludlow Avenue. I suggested she come by. She said she'd meet me on Ludlow; she was busy with something there. There was an edge to her voice that I heard but didn't connect to anything in particular.

When I got to Ludlow, dressed in my indigo cotton sweater vest and gray shorts, I saw Betsy on the north side of the street. Betsy was short, with dark brown curly hair, a handsome, rugged face, and a welcoming smile. I had known her for nearly twenty years. We first met when she played music at gatherings of mental health clients. While I was finishing my bachelor's degree downtown in the late eighties, I frequented Arnold's Bar and Grill on Eighth Street, where she played music on Wednesday nights. Betsy played violin, guitar and sang. She wrote songs, too. In the nineties, when I worked in radio, I often played songs from her album on the radio. Later, when I did social work, we had some clients in common. She worked at Christ Hospital then as a music therapist. We did our studying for the Certified Chemical Dependency Counselor exam at the same time. The day of our written exam in Columbus, we sat side-by-side, and she helped me with some last-minute preparation in the examination hall before the tests were circulated. We both passed that day. After the exam, we lunched together at a Chinese restaurant in Columbus.

Betsy had a blond policewoman with her.

"Steve," Betsy said. "What's going on?"

"I'm on my way to pay bills at the Post Office." I walked with her to the corner.

"I heard about the incident in Sitwell's."

I was stunned. "Okay. Well, it was illegal, that girl smoking in the non-smoking section."

"But I heard how you treated her. That's not you, Steve."

"Betsy, you weren't there. I have to go pay my bills."

"This is Officer Dana," she said. "She wants to talk to you about the incident at the street fair."

"Are you detaining me? I have to pay my bills."

"Will you talk to us afterward?"

"Sure, yeah, okay," I said.

I crossed Ludlow, walked down Ormond to the Post Office. It was a sunny day, so I took off my clip-ons as I came into the dark room. I was trembling with nervousness. I could see Betsy and the policewoman standing outside through the Venetian blinds. Betsy had her official photo I.D. hanging around her neck on a lanyard. I waited in line. Once I got to the front, I asked for the money orders. Bob wasn't there. There were two strangers working. I had to show I.D. and sign my name on a list because I had so much cash. Filling out the money orders was a struggle because I was so scared. I found out a month later, when I got my mail, that I had sent the wrong money orders to the wrong credit card bills, and I put one bill in the envelope so that the address didn't show through the window.

When I came out into the light, I clipped my sunglasses back on. The officer and Betsy followed me to the corner. I wanted to just walk away.

"Steve, are you taking your medication?"

"I'm on a new medication, Betsy. It's different, but it's not bad. I haven't broken any laws."

"What about shouting obscenities at the owner of Sitwell's?" the policewoman asked.

"It's not illegal to call someone a bitch," I said.

"It can be," she said.

"You're standing there in an intimidating stance, with your hand on your gun, and you weren't there in any of the situations. Lisa and I had a difference of opinion," I said.

"But that's not like you," said Betsy.

"Betsy, how do you know? You weren't there."

"I know you, Steve. You don't curse at people or throw tomatoes at them. You don't push people in restaurants." Betsy looked up at me, her lips twisted with concern. She squinted behind her sunglasses, reached up, took them off, and gave me a deep, compassionate look.

"I didn't push anyone. All I did was roll a tomato up the street. This has been blown way out of proportion. I'm crossing here," I said, and started across Ludlow.

They followed.

"Steve, why don't you come with us to the hospital."

"Why? I don't need to go to the hospital."

"Please," said Betsy.

"I'm not trying to intimidate you," said the policewoman.

"No handcuffs," I said.

"No handcuffs."

The patrol car was in the lot next to Habeñero's. They put me in the back seat. I watched Betsy through the metal screen; she turned her head to listen to me as I said, "Thanks for not making me wear handcuffs." People waited at bus stops, walked on Jefferson Avenue, and drove past us as if nothing at all was wrong. We went to University Hospital. I was scared. I wondered if this was the fate of longhaired hippie freaks who scared girls. Betsy led me into the Psychiatric Emergency area. She left me in a room with a steel-wheeled bed and an upholstered chair.

35

Paranoia or Hate Campaign

I TOLD HER SHE should resign now. "Go home, Jean. You've made too many mistakes." She had made too many mistakes to cover them all. I had cadged a stale ham sandwich and a plastic peel-foil-top grape juice at the Formica nursing island in the center of the room. The room was twenty-five feet across and sterile. A round-faced, dark-skinned teenage girl threw her water on me. She waved her arms like a bad actress. I hardly reacted. Jean sent me back to my room and called the techs on the black girl. "Jean, she didn't need to be sedated. You didn't need all that muscle." Jean was an old lady, at least in her fifties, with close-cropped curly gray hair, rectangular wire-rims, a pudgy torso, and small jowls. Her mouth vacillated between a compunctious grin and a flat concerned line. I could see her chin quiver from across the room. A younger nurse in scrubs, pregnant, with shoulder-length dark hair and Jewish features, told me to stay in the quiet room. There were several rooms with heavy deadbolt doors and wired glass mini-windows. Each room had a moveable stainless steel bed along one wall. I sat in an upholstered chair by the bed in my room with my door open. A fluorescent lamp emitted a buzzing sound, making it impossible to relax. The younger woman didn't stay long. Soon Jean was moving around going to the computer. She looked like she was in over her head. "Give up, Jean. Resign. Resign, now. Don't do it," I said.

Two Cincinnati uniforms came with gloves on.

"Will you take your gun belts off?"

"NO."

"Will the two policemen take off their gloves?"

"Okay."

"Will you shake hands?"

The one police officer, the black man who was built like a bodybuilder, did. "Happy to," he said. He had a happy face, good white teeth, wide lips, and a flat nose.

The other, crewcut white boy, wearing little oval wire-rims, jaw shadowed by beard stubble, stood near me.

"You have a hard-on!" I said. His pants bulged. They moved on me. The two cops and the three security officers in blue shirts and black pants attacked. One had a thin face, strawberry blond spiked hair, built and structured like the bartender at Arnold's with the beard and ponytail. They could have been brothers. He was the nicest of the three, but mean, too. The black one had light chocolate skin and was roly-poly fat. I didn't say anything, but he pushed my head into the wall for no reason. The other was white and nondescript. He vanished from memory. The tender's brother replaced my glasses, or sort of did; it was as if they replaced themselves. These three goons did not seem real. I think they may have been part of my hallucination.

It was then that I sensed I had psychokinesis and was calling the shots. Why? I didn't know why I did this to myself. I could never understand it. Antagonism no one needs. They strapped me down, took me upstairs after injecting the drug of choice into my left arm. I was sure it was Geodon, but they claimed it was Haldol and something for alcohol withdrawal. They thought I had been drinking. I had not.

The week before I was taken in, I walked a long walk in Clifton. On Calhoun St., next to the University of Cincinnati campus, I saw signposts with "Kill the Hippies" stenciled on them.

A thin, Waspy man, with a bad crewcut that flared in front like the spoiler on a Trans-Am, buggy eyes, a bit of a hunch to his shoulders, and braces on his over forty-year-old teeth, came in and sat down in the chair by the bed. He held a piece of paper, a list of his patients, in one hand, a pen in the other. I offered him my hand to shake, and he ignored my gesture.

"Mr. Lansky? It smells in here."

I thought of explaining the shoes . . . the shoes I'd hiked into the lake with early in the morning, in the dark, the silt, the socks so many days without washing. Instead, "Do you brush your teeth?" I asked.

"Yes," he said, timidly.

"After every meal?"

"Yes."

"Do you use mouthwash?"

"Yes." Cautiously.

"Would you like a kiss?"

A grimace, a shake of the head, a note of anguish. He started to say something . . . or did he? After that, I grinned, and the interview was over.

36

Hospital Days

EVERY MORNING WE HAD "goal group," and I consistently said, "My goal today is to stay sober." It was all I could manage. We also had to say our names. One morning, one of the other patients, a young, black man with beard stubble and a charming, tremulous voice, introduced himself to the group, saying, "My name is Emerson Dalrymple, and today I'm going to work on my writing."

When my turn came, I said, "My name is Emerson Dalrymple, and today I'm going to work on my writing." The roomful of dazed mental patients, all twenty or so, mostly women, and most of them pregnant, laughed aloud. Emerson laughed, too, and after the meeting called me Emerson. The staff then canceled all my privileges for the day because the privileges were extended to Steve Lansky, not Emerson Dalrymple. I kept refusing the oral Haldol.

I watched tennis and read John Updike. The novel, *Marry Me*, involving love relationships, was sexy, erotic, and complex. I tried to talk to one of the young female staff about it, explicating sentences after reading them to her. She got some of it but seemed embarrassed. After talking with her for only a few minutes in the solarium while the US Open doubles were on, she grew uncomfortable and left the room. For a few days, I imagined that she and I were going to escape and go to New York to play in the mixed doubles together. She was a short, cute, blond with a little turned-up nose and blue eyes. There was another aide who took blood pressure and was also young. I showed her a magic trick on the counter by the phone opposite the nursing station. It involved flipping coins. I explained that it worked better under incandescent lights than fluorescents. I asked her why? She guessed that they flickered at a different speed. She was bright. There was a very dark-skinned, pregnant aide. I talked to her about raising children. I approached her slowly, and cautiously at first. We became friends. I recited my *Fisher* poem for her.

> The abacus beads were
> clunking. A Shawandasset squatted,
> grinned, ate many catfish.
> A Miami clan ate catfish
> gleaned from a little loon lake.
> A duck disappeared.

She said I was a genius. There was a large, light-skinned, black nurse who was very angry with me. I finally sat down near her and told her that I was angry, too. She wanted me to leave her alone. No, I told her, I'm angry, and you have to accept that. She got up and left, but after that, she tolerated me. One of the other nurses wore white sneakers in early September. I started many conversations with her in the hallway as she sat monitoring. I might just talk about anything for a while. Then, as if in a huff, smiling, I would say to her, "D—don't you know it's bad fashion to wear white shoes after Labor Day?" I must have said that to her thirty times. After a while, she said it with me, and we laughed together. One of the late-night staff was an athletic, young, black woman with a long single braid. Once, she braided my hair for me. I told her about my many cycling exploits. Talking to her, I wanted to embellish, make myself the winner and the hero in every story. Sadly, in truth, I never won a single bike race.

I had been playing pranks with the telephones. Every few days, I took the voice element out of the phone in the kitchen and tossed it in a drawer. Then I watched other patients answer the phone. They would talk and soon realize that the phone wasn't working right. I watched two different women talking into the phone, saying, "This phone isn't working." But the staff never seemed to catch on. I disabled the phone in the morning and fixed it in the evening. Things were sufficiently chaotic that no one knew what I had done.

I took a long cold drink of water from the fountain before sitting at the phone across from the glassed-in nursing station with the med-counter opposite. I wanted to be the first call of the morning to the mental health agency where I had worked for nine years until 1997. It was Tuesday, September 11, and the worker I reached knew my case and me.

"I want to restart my disability. I'm in University Hospital's COAC Unit."

"Steve, that's Social Security. We can't do that. You have to call Social Security. I can't help you."

"Are you sure?" I asked.

"Yes. You were on Social Security Disability."

"Thanks," I said, "Goodbye." I felt hostile. I don't know if it came across to the person on the other end of the call. I thought I was being polite. I might have insisted for a minute that the agency was responsible. I hung up the phone and walked down the hall, watching the monitoring devices. There was some meter on the wall with a needle gauge; I think it picked up sound. In the solarium at the end of the hall, the TV was on. As I sat down, I saw Regis Philbin saying something about the World Trade Center. Jet planes were crashing into the towers. What's a movie doing at this hour? I thought. I watched for a while, sort of fascinated.

I started to believe it was real. By calling the agency and demanding disability, I had commenced the attack. I had called in this attack. Finally, I thought. Those bastards are going to pay. Then I thought for a minute and followed the news as it unfolded with news anchors and reporters on the scene. I watched George W. Bush make a statement after talking to elementary kids. I couldn't understand why he was in Florida, nor why he was with kids. Then, in a flash, I could see it. He wanted to be out of harm's way. He had called in these strikes to blame them on an enemy that he wanted to attack. I wondered if maybe the first jet was foreign enemies but the second was Bush. Actually, I was sure of it.

Then, as the rhetoric started, I listened. Something about anyone harboring terrorists was an enemy of the United States. I realized that I was an enemy of George W. Bush. Did that mean that my captors and monitors were harboring me? I puzzled over this. The verisimilitude of the hospital staff and other patients blurred into the scene on the TV. A young African American male patient was talking about terrorists and how much he hated George W. Bush. But I pointed out that I was Bush's enemy and this hospital was holding me. The man walked away, down the hall. He had been sitting on the blue carpet floor, practicing some sort of martial arts stretches. Now, he was moving away from me. I had scared him away.

After hearing about the other two jetliners, I was transfixed. The Pentagon had been hit. This was quite a strike. I was impressed. I remembered the Vietnam War protests on TV and how the Pentagon had then been a target of the anti-war movement. This time it had been hit. There was a jet that might have targeted the White House.

I called my mother from the phone in the solarium. I hadn't talked to her in weeks, didn't think she knew where I was. She was dying of cancer. The last time we had talked, she had cried. I hadn't known what to say to her. My father had been screening my calls. Somehow, this time, I got through. She said, "Steve? Are you okay?"

"Yes. I'm in University Hospital. What's happening?"

"I don't know," she whispered.

"I have to go," I said.

I went to the kitchen phone, put the element back in, and called my friend Karen. I knew I owed Karen an apology. I left a message for her. "Karen, it's Steve Lansky. I'm sorry I was mean to you. I'm in University Hospital on the COAC Unit. I need your help. I need a copy of today's and yesterday's *New York Times.*" I left a number.

A month before, when she was working at the ice cream parlor on the corner of Telford and Ludlow, while I had been marching and playing my bugle outside to protest being banned from Sitwell's Coffeehouse, I talked to her.

"Karen, you don't belong here," I said.

She was smoking a cigarette. I scowled. "What is it, Steve?" she asked.

"You're killing yourself. What are you doing, wasting your life? Smoking cigarettes and working at a shithole?" I walked away while she puffed, looking sad.

I wanted *The New York Times* for September 10th and September 11th. I called a United Dairy Farmer's near campus, and they agreed to hold one of each for me. Now, I needed someone who could pick them up and bring them to me.

One thing I remembered about Karen. Even if the staff was screening my calls, or if another patient answered, Karen would make sure I got the call. Karen was a professional communicator. We had exchanged emails when I had been in Russia, and she had been in California. She spent a summer working in a coffeehouse in Marin County during the time I went to St. Petersburg for a writing seminar, and she'd saved my life by keeping me believing in myself. That summer, she opened the shop every morning and learned to be responsible. Because Karen was a bit chubby, she sometimes didn't have much confidence. But her hazel eyes were pretty and full of life, and she gave the warmest bear hugs and was a fan of my writing. Once, we'd stayed up all night at a great artsy warehouse party. She was kind of a hero to me. And I knew if she forgave me, I would be grateful.

Someone called me to the phone. Karen had called back. "Steve, how are you?" she asked. Her voice was soft, gentle.

"Karen, thanks for calling. Are you okay?"

"What's going on, bub?"

"Crazy day, huh," I said. "I'm with the normal people in here."

"It's strange," she said. "How long have you been there?"

"Since the end of August."

"I wish I were in the hospital." Her voice sounded meek.

"No, you don't, Karen. Trust me, you don't. The food is okay, but this place is full of crazy people." I asked her about school. She was studying French at the University of Cincinnati. "Are you taking classes?"

"They start in two weeks."

"My thesis defense was canceled because I'm locked in here. They won't let me call my advisor or my committee members because it's a long-distance call."

"Oh, Steve."

"Karen, I'm a mess."

"No, you're in a safe place."

"You think?"

"Yes."

"Did you get copies of the *Times*?"

"Not yet."

"I called the UDF off Calhoun, and they're holding both issues for me."

"Okay."

"Can you bring them?"

"Are you allowed to have visitors?"

"Yes, I think so."

"I'll come this afternoon."

"Karen, you're the best. I'm sorry I was mean to you."

"No. It's okay. Hang in there." Her voice reassured me. I needed Karen to be my friend. You can't imagine how much it meant to me that she showed up that afternoon. She brought me an ice cream sundae and two issues of *The New York Times*. I know now that I was still crazy, that my thoughts were disorganized. Karen hugged me. We shed a tear together, and she sat with me in my room while we talked. She wore a chocolate brown sweater, a dark skirt, and black leggings. Her hair was pulled back with berets.

"George W. Bush wants to be the next baseball Czar. They canceled Major League Baseball. Now, that was a power play. He goes from being a team owner to the White House, but now he's taking over baseball. How is this going to affect the trade deadline? Does he think the World Trade Center is about baseball trades? Did you know that he's trying to outdo Kenesaw Mountain Landis?"

"Who?" Karen asked.

"I'm glad you asked," I said. "When I drive from Cincinnati to Oxford, I go through Millville, Ohio, a town so small that it has two traffic lights—if you blink, you miss it. There's a sign outside Millville that says: Birthplace of Kenesaw Mountain Landis First Baseball Czar, Born 1866. If you glance up quickly while driving by, it looks like it says, "Ladies First Baseball Czar.""

"What's a baseball Czar?"

"That's what they used to call the baseball commissioner," I laughed. "But there's no ladies' baseball league in America. George W. wouldn't allow it."

Karen made a funny face. I sat in the Naugahyde and wooden chair facing my window. "Can I sit on the empty bed?" Karen asked. At the time, I didn't have a roommate.

"Sure."

She sat on the white sheets and bounced and grinned.

"Karen, be good," I said.

She laughed.

One of the staff was walking by my door and saw Karen in the room. "Steve, you're not supposed to have visitors in your room," she said. When she saw that Karen was on the vacant bed, she said, "Now I'll have to change those sheets."

Karen hugged me and left. "I'll be back," she said.

Over the next few days, I pored over the newspapers. Some of the things that I noticed: On September 10, there was a full-page advertisement on page A19 from the Anti-Defamation League. The ad stated: "Anti-Semitism. It's not a History Lesson; it's a Current Event. The UN World Conference Against Racism in Durban turned into a hate forum against the State of Israel and the Jewish People. To those who stood in solidarity with us, we say, "Thank you." Thank you, President George W. Bush.... Thank you, Secretary of State Colin Powell.... Thank you, to all the good people who condemned the hijacking of the World Conference Against Racism and the singling out of the democratic State of Israel. Together, we will continue the fight against anti-Semitism and racism at home and abroad with civility, respect, and cooperation."

Also, on the tenth, on page C6, a quarter-page advertisement that might have appeared any day but seemed poignant because of the photograph with it. All of lower Manhattan shown from offshore in the air, a skyline dominated by the World Trade Center's Twin Towers with block lettering: THIS IS OUR CAMPUS in the foreground. It was an ad for NYU's Executive Programs.

Another political advertisement from the tenth, on page D5, on the bottom fourth of the page: "War in the Middle East Can it happen? How can it be avoided?" Paid for by FLAME, Facts, and Logic About the Middle East, it began: "The Arab uprising in Israel, the "Al Aksa Intifada," has now been going on since September of last year. Hundreds have died, and thousands have been wounded. What is happening has all the earmarks of a civil war. But it isn't just the Palestinians that Israel is confronted with. All of the Arab world and Iran are backing the Palestinians and are goading them on. Any spark could trigger a full-fledged war—which, in all likelihood, would result in all of the Arab states and Iran lined up against Israel." The ad went on to advocate that Israel put down any "uprising" with deliberate speed and force.

The headline of the Sports Section that Monday, September 10, read: "The Jets' New Chapter Goes Back for an Instant Rewrite" A coincidence, of course, as everyone knows the Jets were a New York NFL team. (As if the jets were the ones that collided with the World Trade Center and history was rewritten.)

Then in Tuesday's paper, on the editorial page: "The Politics of Panic." On page D1, the Science Times, "Protect Sharks? Attacks Fuel Old Argument" and in the International news on page A11: "Reports Disagree on Fate of Anti-Taliban Rebel Chief," an article detailing a suicide bombing in Afghanistan on September 9, which is equivocal on whether Ahmed Shah Massoud survived the attack.

When I turned to the Arts section, there were two headlines that caught my attention. Again, I'm sure it was only coincidence, as this sort of rhetoric was common to any journalistic product. An article about a memoir by one of the radical "Weather Underground." "No Regrets for a Love of Explosives" read the headline on page B1. If you looked at the bottom of the same page, there was a headline that foreshadowed an American political position: "Pleased to Offend, France's Shock Novelist Strikes Again." Given Karen's study of the French language and my interest in shock novels, this one seemed fun. But in the days to come, the French would be maligned for allegedly offending America.

So, looking at all this from the *Times*, I was sure that something strange was in the works. I took it a step further. As far as I knew, something about Pfizer Inc. was part of the equation. Later I saw the film and read the book about John Nash, the celebrated economist who was also schizophrenic. His disease included hallucinations that suggested specific messages were coming to him from newspaper headlines. I was not a Nobel-winning mathematician, but I could see that Pfizer contributed to an art show at the Philadelphia Museum of Art that was advertised in the Tuesday paper, September 11, 2001. The ad showed a photo of a pair-oared shell rendered in 1872. Pfizer manufactures Geodon, the medication I needed, and which I wanted to keep taking instead of Haldol. This ad, with Pfizer Inc., as a corporate supporter, demonstrated a support of elite sports and art. These coincided with my own values. Hadn't I just made a major bicycle ride that would have been impossible on Haldol? Wasn't the editorial on September 10, 2001, on page A30, entitled: "An Unhealthy Influence on Doctors," an indication that doctors were susceptible to the persuasive efforts of pharmaceutical monetary pressures? I had seen pens with advertising from Olanzapine and Zoloft, but Geodon's maker, Pfizer, just wasn't giving enough. I was preparing a court case to prove I had my faculties about me. I wanted a lawyer to support my side of the story about what had happened in Sitwell's over the girl smoking in the non-smoking area. I had no idea that I was out of line. I took any information and turned it into evidence for my righteous indignation.

I called a family friend who worked with my mother. She was a lawyer. I talked to her. She was one of my mom's best friends. She was nice. I talked to her daughter. All's well. Take the Haldol or go to PWLC, the state hospital. I guess it's PWLC, 'cause I don't want the Haldol. She took my poll and said there should be no smoking in all restaurants.

Did she know that my incident was over smoking?

As long as I argued the facts, I could not win the case. I had to concede all the facts and agree I was crazy.

I talked to the lawyer they sent me. He didn't want to help me present my case. I wanted to read from an editorial in the NYT about pharmaceutical companies pushing certain drugs and from an advertisement that promoted art and culture with an older photo of a racing shell and read the list of sponsors to get to Pfizer. Pfizer made Geodon. I wanted to state my whole case, explain the incident. He discouraged me. When they next came to take me to court, I didn't go. They gave me some sloppily Xeroxed forms and told me I had lost. They force-medicated me.

Another morning at goal group in the square room with two walls of windows, I asked, "Who killed buddy gray?" (buddy gray was a Cincinnati activist who worked and lived in Over-the-Rhine and was killed by a man he was trying to help rehabilitate.) They came with security guards to strap me down. I walked with them down the hall after a serious talk with one of the men who were ready to fight me. His brother was a famous local jazz guitarist, and we had talked about friends in common. That day he said, "Just doing my job."

"I won't forget," I said. "Follow your heart."

One afternoon I begged my social worker to let me go outside with an escort to smoke a cigarette. I stood in the hallway by the nurses' station shouting, "I call the question. Let's have a vote. The only one who won't let me go out to smoke is the doctor. He's outvoted. Isn't this a democracy? I want a cigarette."

My social worker took me into a little carpeted meeting room. He told me he was going on vacation. He said he knew I didn't smoke. He said there was no way I was going out to smoke. I was angry because so many of the staff smoked, and I figured that my "crime" was being an anti-smoking zealot. No wonder they were against me. He said, "There are seven things you need." Then he wrote the word Haldol on a paper towel seven times. I launched into a whole delusion that Geodon cost the same as a pack of cigarettes a day and that Haldol cost about one cigarette. They were trying to force me to buy this less expensive cigarette, and it had something to do with Communism versus Democracy. Now, as I write this, I cannot recapture the logic. I explained it to several people, but no one ever got the argument. Seven Haldol had the value of one cigarette.

The three goons who first knocked me down appeared days later after the buddy gray thing. I took the meds orally that time. They didn't put their hands on me; just lounged against the wall, in the doorway, tilting their heads and touching their pants with hands that looked moist. It might have been a hallucination. One asked me if I was an English professor. I acknowledged that.

"Where?"

"Miami University."

This was University Hospital. The University of Cincinnati. They had mean voices. I took the liquid concentrate Haldol. Bitter. This was after being escorted to the quiet room where I lay back and waited for them to see how calm I was. They used only two-point restraints this time. Soon, I was allowed to go back to my bedroom to sleep the day away. Man, that stuff made me drowsy.

On the buddy gray day, the male nurse who psychoanalyzed me gave me the shots. This man had a look kind of like Jeff Bridges in *The Big Lebowski*. He thought he was the best. I think he was an underachiever who beat up on people to build his ego. I told him I had sex with a dog once. Some patients overheard. He wanted to prove that this had shamed me. One night I asked to talk to him. He took me into a room, and I told him I heard voices. He asked if they were inside my head or outside. I pretended I thought they were outside, jerking my head around. I told him the graduate program was too high-pressure and competitive, and I didn't have any friends. I was lying. Acting. I began to cry, working myself into quite a state. He consoled me, but I jerked away from his touch. That part was real.

When he injected me, he wasn't that good, I could hear his breathing, and he had to get dramatic with the syringe in his mouth sideways, while he cotton swabbed the left arm. I thought I heard a rumor that buddy's killer had been on the COAC Unit before he was released and killed buddy. I might have heard it in my head.

My friend Mike came to visit and said, "Take the Haldol. Cooperate." He had known buddy gray. Mike was a thin man in his fifties with a thick shock of gray hair. He had a handsome face, deep blue eyes, and he wrote novels and poetry. Mike was one of my best friends. He was the best man at my wedding. He also talked with me and supported my decision to leave my ex. I asked him who killed buddy, and he told me, "Wilbur D...." Mike gave me a copy of *King Lear* and sat with me. I showed him some writings I was working on. He visited from the beginning. Other friends came to visit, and Nurse Dude said, "I thought you said you didn't have any friends."

The last time was the best. I lay down in the hallway entry to my room, falling backward as they held me up. I wanted to force them to drag me. Dwayne got it (Dwayne was cool. He was good-looking in an everyday way, but a bit pudgy. He had confidence. The day we first met, I gave him some shit, and he told me he wasn't going to take it and I could go to the quiet room. I walked to the quiet room, and when he asked me to empty my pockets, I threw all my change on the floor. He said if I thought he was going to pick that up, I was really nuts. I apologized, picked up the change, and we reached a tentative understanding. Later, I tried to introduce him to a friend at the radio station, but Dwayne wasn't working the day she came to visit me). I started to pray for them, and chant Harë Krishna, and he said it was "a kind of passive resistance thing." I said, "Do me right here." The oral Haldol wasn't enough for them. They chatted and agreed. The security guys stood and watched. I prayed out loud for the ones I knew, using their names, and then read the nametags of the others and prayed for their mortal souls. One of the guards was pleased that I pronounced his name correctly. Dwayne did both arms. Then I got up and went back to bed. From then on, the drugs took hold.

I called my old case manager, Carl, at home. He listened to me. I think he said he was glad to hear I was getting back to my old self. He came to visit once while I was taking a bath. We talked through the bathroom door. He decided to come back later. We had a conversation where he told me I had said many outrageous things to the women staff at the hospital. I must have said that the women should wear their hair down and uncut, that they should wear dresses or skirts and blouses, and should not polish their nails or toenails. I had said that women should serve me. Carl said I was described as if I was a character that Andy Kaufman played on Taxi, Latka's alter ego, Tony Cliff, a sort of sleazy womanizer who had no regard for women's views, opinions, or common sense. I was baffled by all this, coming from Carl. I could remember some interactions when I had been on the Geodon, the first several days, but I had no idea I had been so rudely intolerant. I know that some of the women who worked on the unit were angry with me, and did not seem to like me. I had apparently treated them with true disdain.

A lot of friends came to visit. At least seven others that I remember. Everyone brought something. I was so happy to have visitors with magazines, cookies, pizza, Indian curry, Stewart's sodas, and books. I loved my friends so much. I talked to many on the phone also. As my senses returned, I found pleasure in talking to a lot of different people. But many of these conversations took place while I was still struggling to come back to sanity. I talked on the phone nearly every night to Niki, who worked the late shift at WNKU. She had just had a child and was struggling with the management over bringing her son and dog to work. Friends like Niki and Karen saved my life. My fellow graduate students were supportive, too. I had not known them as long, and my closest friends had become a bit weary because I had been so difficult with them in recent interactions, but they came back over when they saw me come back to sanity.

Obviously, because there was no understanding on my part, I just couldn't understand why everyone was out to get me. To get me on Haldol. I didn't like Haldol. It knocked me out physically. I had so much less energy hours after taking it. But it had become starkly clear that to live in the world, I had to take it. I knew that now—even if the siren call of Geodon energy was still strong.

The adventures on it had been exhilarating in their way, and partly because of that, and partly because of the shame, the coming back after being away was the hardest thing I'd ever experienced. It's unbearable to describe the shame. I had been intolerant and mean to those I loved, and that was nearly impossible to forgive myself for or accept.

Journal entry:

> Autumn 12:20 p.m. 9/23/01
> leaves scatter, rustle, breeze
> ch-ch in anima ear
> supple stems, cattails
> frown, frowsy, fronds, frisky,
> frizzle, friend. Where is
> my duster, my blue paint?
> Steven Paul Lansky
> University Hospital
> Incarcerated—still no pass

***

Days have passed since then. I'm free. I'm so on Haldol. I feel as though my head has been kicked down a stair. It's not exactly that I hurt, it's just that the energetic physical part of me, the part that had my churning legs motoring a Skycycle one hundred and twenty-four miles along the Loveland trail a little over a month ago, is now dormant. Now I can't handle more than a dozen sit-ups, and my appetite is weird. In the first weeks at UC hospital, amid the dead decor, the lack of plant life, the willingness to act any way at all to please a certain nurse or convince him that I was getting better, I did sixty sit-ups a day. Sometimes two sets of thirty, other days three sets of twenty. Then, I had drive. I masturbated vigorously, standing in the shared bathroom in the wee hours to sap enough spirit to let me sleep. I spurted jism into the bell of the toilet, wiped up the excess with a tissue, and slept in my clothes. For the first ten days, I had no change of clothes. Every day I would wash my Volvo Cannondale socks and my Hanes briefs in the sink or shower. The doctor said I stank and refused to shake my hand. It was a dark time. Friends visited, and I spun tales. My head may have been paranoid and schizo, but my body was fit. I was a forty-three-year-old man of masculine pride and heat. What was I off the Geodon? That, I'm afraid, is harder to say.

Epilogue

WHEN I THINK BACK on those *Darke County Days* now, over
twenty years later, I can see how fortunate I was and am. I even
feel fortunate to have had those days, as they give me a sense
of contrast. That sense began almost right away after I started
back on Haldol and got out of the hospital. I spent the month
of September 2001 in University Hospital in Cincinnati being
reintroduced to antipsychotic meds. I've been essentially stable
on them ever since. One of my first tasks, upon getting back
into my apartment and taking care of laundry which another
tenant in the building had pulled from the washing machine and
dumped, wet, in a plastic garbage bag in the basement, involved
following up with the Darke County Court system. I arranged
for a court date. If I remember correctly it was early November
when I drove there.

In preparation for the visit, I took some of my writings that
had been published in zines, and I went to the Big Sky Bakery
in Clifton, a few blocks from my apartment, to buy muffins that I
planned to give, along with the zines, to the Deputies following
the hearing. I didn't want to offer anything to influence anyone,
but I wanted to reconnect with the authorities, who, in the end,
had treated me quite civilly.

After driving gently curving and banking country roads with
the sunroof open, I reached Greenville, Ohio. That clear,
crisp, fall day found me talking with the assistant prosecutor. I
apologized for the behavior that had led to my arrest. I added
that I didn't mean to scare anyone. I told the well-dressed
gentleman with the smell of office and cologne, that I had a
mental illness and I'd spent a month getting back on the right

meds, and now I was taking care of the wreckage that I had created in my decompensated state.

Specifically, I said what a lawyer friend had suggested. "I throw myself on the mercy of the court. I want to make good on whatever damage I have caused."

The prosecutor responded by telling me that he would drop the charge of parking illegally on the edge of the roadway and let me plead guilty to the charge of fleeing and eluding police officers. He would recommend to the court that I serve a few additional days in jail (I had served six), pay a fine, and do community service. I don't remember the total amount of the fine, but it was substantial for a graduate student.

Then I went before the judge. The courtroom was as I had remembered, though this time without any cameras. I remembered the judge from when I tossed the wadded-up piece of paper onto his desk. I apologized to him, both personally and professionally. I spoke clearly and precisely, admitting to the crimes and asking for the court's mercy. He responded by sentencing me to time served, a fine a little less than the prosecutor had recommended, and community service. I think it was one or two hundred hours and I had some months to complete it. He said I could meet with the probation officer in Darke County and arrange to do the community service in Cincinnati. He was quite kind and reasonable.

I met the officer after court, and he too spoke gently and reasonably. He suggested I could call once I found a community service location, and once the supervisor and he spoke briefly on the phone, I could fax my time sheets weekly until I'd met the total number of hours, after which I'd be cleared.

Then I went out to the jail facility and found Corporal Tom and Josh, both of whom were quite kind. They accepted the muffins, teasingly saying, "You aren't trying to poison us, are you, Steve?"

We talked in the lobby area of the jail. They couldn't let me into the processing room. The day was warm enough that we stood in the sunshine that filtered through the glass doors until we all felt comfortable and then stood outside in the fresh air talking. I gave them some copies of my writings, and we all shook hands.

Josh laughed and told me, "I remember once you asked if you could hold the key to the jail." I hadn't remembered that but later worked it into my write-up. He could not have been more pleasant.

Corporal Tom seemed a bit more distant but concluded, "We knew right away you weren't like most of our customers." He said maybe he would come down to Cincinnati for a cup of coffee sometime to see me. I said he would be welcome.

No salamanders crawled out from under the rocks in the rock garden out front. I heard no cows lowing in the afternoon breeze. The low brick building seemed out of place and disorienting, not at all the way it had been that first night when they brought me in from my wrecked car. Today the car ran well. I drove home and resolved to do the community service soon, so it would not linger into the time allowed. My mother's health had taken a turn for the worse, and my father hardly spoke to me because of the things I had said and done while off the meds. He had a difficult time understanding that I'd meant nothing personally and that I still loved him and Mother, despite my having been in a psychotic state some months before. I longed for some sort of better understanding within my family circle.

Resolved to finish the community service without complications, I called a friend. He suggested the Lower Price Hill Community School. He got me an appointment to meet the director, a busy man who seemed always between phone calls and ensconced in a big, well-lit office with a wide wooden conference table, a massive desk, and an active school all around him. He wore a tie with a white shirt, had a firm handshake, and when I told him that I needed to do community service, he didn't ask a lot of questions, called the probation officer, and within two weeks we were in business. I would spend my required hours in the school tutoring GED students or students who had just finished their GED's and were going to Cincinnati State Community College. I could make lunch from the supplies in the kitchen, read books from the available library, as long as I was available to tutor on-demand while I was there.

Soon, it became apparent that there were very few students who needed tutoring at any given time. Needing something with which to occupy me, I found a copy of *The Grapes of Wrath* lying around. The thick book with its worn pages, numbers nestled in the corners, hard binding, dry and scented with the scent of old book, felt solid in my large hand. I hefted it from hand to hand.

It fell open to chapter three. I read the short chapter about the turtle crossing the highway with the burrs, seeds, cement ridges, humorous eyes, and protruding feet.

The description fed me. It filled the spot that had been aching ever since this whole ordeal began back on Highway 127 last summer when I stopped my car at night and sat puzzled until the policeman came up behind me. I flipped back to the beginning of the book and found the dust, the dry, the corn, the wind, the insects, the grasshoppers, all the details built around a story that in chapter two got quickly but not too quickly to the troubled Tom Joad who was just getting out of prison, and I saw in a new way something I had known, and it was the satisfaction of a book. The heft, the chemistry of my fingers and hands on wide paper, the ink that left the imprint of John Steinbeck's notions for me was just the answer. And as it all turned out I came day after day to the Lower Price Hill Community School until I'd served my community service in full and I had read *The Grapes of Wrath* from front cover to back cover and back again. Tutoring individuals from time to time was easy.

Back in the den of my apartment, I sat and composed a long-overdue letter to Lisa, Sitwell's owner, taking responsibility for the smoking incident and my part in offending Lock's friend. In a separate letter that I wrote to Lock at Lisa's suggestion, I apologized to him and his friend. Things were awkward at first, but gradually people began to see that I had returned to my old self. Lisa understood mental illness better than most. I was lucky in that. I thanked her for her willingness to go to court and help get me back on Haldol.

Once I began to write the account you now hold in your hands, the pain of having to face my darkness and my illness proved instrumental in keeping me grounded. Lisa teased me about my affliction in a gentle way, as friends do, and I found it therapeutic to be able to laugh at what my crazy dysfunctional behavior had sometimes led me to do.

Once it became clear that Lacey wasn't interested in me romantically, our friendship lost steam, though we didn't lose touch entirely. She began to work at Contemporary Dance Theatre in North College Hill, where many of my other friends performed in dance, performance art, and music. In early 2002, a mutual acquaintance, a professor at the University of Cincinnati who had studied at the University of Iowa, was making a short film and recruited the two of us separately to be extras in a scene shot in the Cincinnati Art Museum. In this case, there were cameras, sound equipment, lighting—but it was a real film not just a product of my imagination.

The morning of the shoot, Lacey and I walked past one another, without speaking, in a gallery where a van Gogh painting hung on an otherwise open wall. Undergrowth with Two Figures. The filmmaker had special permission to include the van Gogh in his film, and the juxtaposition of the figures in the woods seemed apropos.

My recollection of that day sadly sticks in the not-the-proudest-moments page of my Lacey memories. But only because we didn't speak. We sat on the corner of a set of stone benches in the lobby, each drinking a soda from a can. I tried to imagine how she felt. She was probably too young to have much understanding of mental illness. I know when I was in my early twenties, and afflicted with schizophrenia, I didn't have much understanding of it. I think she thought I objectified her, but also knew I was a friend.

Years later, she spread her wings, moved to San Francisco, chatted online with me about dating, wrote a blog about dating and addiction, and found work as a teacher. She gained a better understanding of me after I shared some of my writings with her. And in her own life, she found love with a man who already had a child (she went on to have another child with him). Whenever I think of Lacey, it is with warmth and affection. Yet I can't deny a pang of sadness, too.

In the late winter of 2002, feeling restored, I faxed my final timesheet to the Darke County probation officer, and then, with a sense of justice served, went back to my family ready to face my angry father, my dying mother, and my distant brother.

Acknowledgments

I have four writing communities that have all contributed to this project: The Zen writing sangha supported my artwork as well. My late aunt Katherine Thanas and her friend, Natalie Goldberg. Thanks also to Neola, Saundra, Dorotea, who listened. The Appalachian writing community with Dennis, Scott, Mike, Dick, Pauletta, Dana, Jim, Owen, James, Robert, Ed, and Gurney. The Tampa community with Misha, Jeff, Josip, Resa, Kevin, Steve, and a handful of others. The Miami community with Keith, Peter, Eric, Cathy, cris, Margaret, Kay, David, Jim, Billy, Bill, Lisa, Andrew, Mary Jean and Andy. This project was not workshopped. I'd like to especially thank the editors and publishers who took sections for newspapers and journals: Arie, Greg, Larry, Phong, Resa and Maria.

Thank you to Peter Alson, who started out as a poker buddy in college, has become a close friend, and has worked tirelessly to refine this book, always with the reader in mind. Thank you, Rachel Ake, for the cover design.

This book would not exist without the many treatment teams that shepherded me through psychiatric hospitalizations successfully. It's clear to me that these hard-working professionals, underpaid staff workers, foodservice, custodial, and security people have bravery, dedication, and humility that puts them often in difficult circumstances with patients who are in precarious mental and emotional conditions, and often present these difficulties in combination with other complex issues regarding physical health. Thankfully I have met those who were willing to give and understand. Mental health workers do God's work for little reward. I hope that psychiatric treatment, and therapy grow progressively more humane. I also want to thank the government officials and office holders who broke bread with the humans who created the Family Medical Leave Act. Without Social Security the mental health system would punish those it now serves. Service and volunteerism along with disability help keep it sane for all of us.

Thank you to Megan Fitze for her help in gaining support in the form of a small grant from the Ohio Arts Council.

Thanks also to family, including Bette, Josselyn, David, William and Suzy. Michael F., thank you for your ongoing efforts to ensure my security. My late parents who would argue that this is my most important book are the shoulders I surely want to stand on. I want to thank my brother, Dave, whose humility and patience are the marks of a lasting friendship. We have not always felt, seen, or heard the same solution, yet we have remained solution oriented.

Made in United States
North Haven, CT
09 February 2023

32249329R00148